75 SECRETS

An Insider's Guide to:
Bank CDs,
Annuities, and
Retirement Planning

BILL HARRIS

President, W.V.H., Inc.

Published by W.V.H., Inc.
San Diego, California

75 SECRETS An Insider's Guide to:
Bank CDs,
Annuities,
and Retirement Planning

Published by
W.V.H., Inc.
10626 Falcon Rim Point
San Diego, California, 92131
www.75secrets.com

2014 Edition - First Printing

Cover Design by John Hamer

ISBN: 978-0984448739
Library of Congress Control Number: 2010924409

Important Message

You will soon learn secrets about Certificates of Deposit, Tax-Deferred Annuities, and about planning for retirement. Some of these secrets took us a career to learn, other secrets evolved from us working with some of the giants in the financial services industry over the last 20 years, and a few special secrets were the result of countless hours of research.

Most of the 75 Secrets are only four pages long: The Secret title page has a short opening paragraph that gives you what you need to know before inviting you to learn more. The second page has up to 300 carefully selected words so you learn as much as possible about the Secret in the least amount of time, but you learn enough about the Secret to discuss it with your advisor for advice. The third page, which is always to the right of the second page, is a visual; at the least, it is a visual summary of what was discussed on the opposite page; at the most, it is a potentially award-winning chart that captures the "heart" of the Secret and the importance of doing something about it before it is too late. The fourth and last page share the Next Steps for you to consider taking.

Speaking of Next Steps, show the appropriate Secret in this book to your tax and/or legal advisor for their opinion. If they concur with our feelings, then reach out to your insurance professional and/or investment professional for their opinion.

Important Message

Why are these steps important? W.V.H., Inc. and its officers and employees are not trained or qualified to provide tax advice and we cannot offer the correct financial advice for you since we do not know you and your circumstances. Your tax and legal advisors and your insurance professional and/or investment professional can determine what is in your best interest.

As you will see in the Table of Contents, a good description of Certificates of Deposit and Tax-Deferred Annuities begins on page 327. Since every financial choice has advantages and disadvantages, we publish some of the advantages and disadvantages of owning Certificates of Deposit and Tax-Deferred Annuities on page 333.

The 30 Short Bonus Secrets beginning on page 307 is our way of under-promising and over-delivering. We promised you 75 Secrets. You are getting 105 Secrets. Since the 30 Bonus Secrets are uniquely short and to the point, this section becomes your way to learn a lifetime of inside information in less than 30 minutes.

Bill Harris
President
W.V.H., Inc.
wvharris@adnc.com
www.75secrets.com

About the Author

Bill Harris is President of W.V.H., Inc.

Bill Harris is the founder of 5 different companies; companies that wrote over 1 billion dollars of annuity premium. Bill has appeared in *Money* magazine and in *The Wall Street Journal*, on TV and radio, in State Superior Court as an annuity expert witness, and "on stage" as one of the most sought after speakers with over 3,000 seminars and web conferences under his belt. Bill is the founder and president of W.V.H., Inc., a consulting and intellectual services company that licenses sales concepts, training tools, and creative media to some of the largest companies in the financial services industry. W.V.H., Inc., has created over 100 CD-ROMs and DVD-ROMs, has published ten books, and has produced many informative short films about the economy, inflation, Social Security, and saving.

Thank You

We would like to thank everyone who made this book possible.

To Ashley Carter and Evan Ponder, thank you for those long meetings at the University of Colorado and for your dedication, caring, and uncanny eye for detail. Both of you made the book special.

To Erica Radke, thank you for being with us from beginning to end.

To Sabrina Vonallmen, thanks for teaching us how to reach out to some of the brightest minds on the CU campus.

To Sherry Tucker for reading all 16 drafts.

To John Hamer, the cover and your initial design layouts were creative magic at its best.

To Nick Gerhart and Frank Marino, thanks for having seasoning and the willingness to be the first to offer constructive criticism.

To Evaleen Minez Harris for her advice about color selection. You know your stuff. W.V.H.,Inc. looks forward to your advice for the next 42 years. Thanks Evaleenie!

To my friends and associates for responding to my pleas for volunteers within minutes of us asking for help. Thanks Jason S., James J., Russ W., James R., Ed L., Paul Mc., and Dan M. You know who you are.

To Susan Humason for helping me with the 1st edition.

To Rosemary Horvath for helping me with all editions and giving me your best and having the patience of a saint. Thanks.

And, thanks to my family, Mary, my wife, my children, Elizabeth, Will, and Chris; Gregory, my son-in-law; and my grandchildren Jackson Harris and Ella Rose for listening to me talk about this book incessantly.

3 Special Secret Contributors

While we are very proud that W.V.H., Inc. authored 72 of the 75 Secrets and all of the 25 Short Bonus Secrets, we reached out to some of the brightest minds in the financial services industry for 3 of the Secrets. Two of the Secret contributors are with two large and highly respected companies in the U.S. The views that they express are solely their views and not necessarily the views of their company.

3 Special Contributors

1. Scott Stolz, Senior Vice President, Private Client Group Investment Products, Raymond James Insurance Group. His contribution is Secret 68: *An excess withdrawal could cancel a major guarantee found in annuities,* and Secret 43: *Lock in a lifetime interest stream at today's low interest rates.*

We all owe Scott a thank you for uncovering an overlooked annuity provision in Secret 68 that can lessen an important guarantee and potentially cost annuity owners thousands of dollars. As a result of Scott's Secret 43, you will learn why now might be the time to lock in a lifetime income stream.

2. John Wesley, Director in Product Management at TIAA-CREF, the oldest issuer of Variable Annuities in the Qualified Market.

Thanks to John for contributing Secret 65 about the Guaranteed Lifetime Withdrawal Benefit. John's experience in building and pricing annuities, his marketing savvy, his honesty, and his willingness to unveil how to evaluate the "real value" of this lifetime withdrawal benefit could help thousands make the right decision. Said differently, we are lucky to know John Wesley.

3. Tim Austgen, CPA, La Jolla, California

Thanks to Tim for Secret 46: *An annuity can lower your Modified Adjusted Gross Income, tax bracket, and get you new tax deductions.* We all owe Tim a thank you for confirming our suspicion that a tax-deferred annuity could offer additional tax advantages for some lucky taxpayers. This Secret could potentially bring more accountants, insurance/investment professionals, and consumers together in one meeting. Also, a BIG thank you to Tim for reviewing tax law as it pertains to Secrets 14, 20, 25, 39, 41, 58 and 63.

Contents

Certificates of Deposit

Contents

Retirement

Contents

Retirement

Contents

Retirement

Contents

Tax-Deferred Annuities

Contents

Tax-Deferred Annuities

Contents

Tax-Deferred Annuities

Contents

2014 Changes and Opportunities

We cannot recall a year in the past where there have been so many changes and opportunities as there have been in 2013 and 2014. Carpe Diem! Below is a summary of 18 changes and opportunities for 2014. The following 4 pages are only a brief summary. Please refer to the pages indicated where more details are provided. Since circumstances do differ from individual to individual and since neither the author or the copyright owner are qualified to offer tax, legal, savings, or investment advice, all parties should consult with their own advisors.

1. Increased Tax Brackets
Effective 2014, there are now 7 Marginal Tax Brackets with the 39.6% tax bracket being the top tax bracket for the 2nd consecutive year. Who will be in the 39.6% tax bracket? Those single taxpayers with incomes exceeding $406,751, head of household taxpayers with incomes exceeding $432,201, and couples filing jointly with incomes exceeding $457,601.

More details including the next steps for you and your tax advisor to potentially reduce your taxable income so you fall into a lower Marginal Tax Bracket are throughout this book.

2. Increased SEP contribution
In 2014, small business owners may slash their income tax liability, build a BIG retirement account, and possibly exclude all or some of their employees by making a 2013 SEP contribution of $52,000.

More details including the benefits to having a Simplified Employee Plan can be found on pages 163-166.

3. Increased 401(k) contribution
In 2013, 401(k) contributions were increased to $17,500 for those age 49 and younger and $23,000 for those age 50 and older under the Catch-Up provision. In 2014, the $17,500 and $23,000 401(k) contribution maximum remains unchanged.

More details including the benefits to taking advantage of a 401(k) and the Catch -Up provision can be found on pages 99-102; details about the power of employer matching can be found on pages 67-70 and pages 313-314.

4. Increased IRA contribution

In 2013, the maximum IRA contribution for those age 49 and younger has been increased for the first time since 2008 to $5,500 and to $6,500 for someone age 50 and older. In 2014, the $5,500 and $6,500 IRA maximum remains unchanged.

5. For the second time ever, the CPI-E, the CPI-U and the CPI-W all showed identical inflation rates in 2012.

In 2013, the CPI-E was 1.6%, the CPI-W was 1.5% and the CPI-U was 1.5%.

More details about lessening the impact of inflation can be found under #7 below.

6. 2013 inflation rate results in the 40 yr average to be 4.36%.

In 2014, more savers will begin to realize that their returns need to exceed inflation. And while inflation in 2013 averaged only 1.5%, more savers have discovered that a) their cost of living was appreciably more than 1.5% and b) their returns need to exceed current Bank CD interest rates since inflation has averaged over 4.3% over the last 40 years.

More details about inflation, the impact of inflation, and potential solutions can be found on pages 21-24, 57-60, 95-98, 103-106, 127-130, 139-142, 187-190.

7. Among elderly Social Security beneficiaries, 23% of married couples and 46% of unmarried persons rely on Social Security for 90% or more of their retirement income.

It is sad, isn't it? However, Social Security was never designed to be one's primary source of income.

Details related to being less dependent on Social Security later are under #11 on the next page. Details for those already receiving Social Security begin under #12.

8. Average monthly benefit for a retired worker in 2013 was $1,269 a month.

While it is too late for some, it may not be too late for you.

Details related to being less dependent on Social Security later are under #11 below; details for those already receiving Social Security begin under #12.

9. Beginning in 2013, the Social Security statement will no longer be mailed but can be accessed online.
In 2014, understanding your Social Security Statement online becomes your new responsibility as a spouse and parent.

Details related to being less dependent on Social Security later are under #11 below; details for those already receiving Social Security begin under #12.

10. There are now 2.8 workers paying in for every Social Security beneficiary.

Details related to being less dependent on Social Security are on pages,41-44, 119-122, 311; Details for those already receiving Social Security begin under #12.

11. New Social Security worksheet
As reported in earlier editions, far too many are paying income taxes unnecessarily on Social Security Income. This 2014 edition includes a special worksheet that will potentially help you get more spendable income by reducing the income taxes you are paying on your Social Security. Perfect worksheet to show your tax advisor.

More details and worksheet can be found on pages 211-214 and on pages 340-341.

12. More research on ways to defer the beginning of Social Security to age 70.
In 2014, more people will reexamine the advantages and disadvantages of electing Social Security to begin at age 66 or 70 instead of age 62.
Details about the 4 things you need to consider are on pages 45-48 and a new alternative is unveiled on page 319.

13. Medicare Surtax now becomes the 6th thing to take into consideration before making a ROTH conversion.
In 2014, a ROTH conversion might be more costly because of the new 3.8% Medicare Surtax.

Details about the ROTH Conversion can be found on pages 53-56 and details on "undoing" a conversion on pages 155-158 including conversions that cannot be "undone" (recharacterization).

14. The "tipping point" might be easier in 2014 after an annuity reduces

the Adjusted Gross Income.

Learn how an annuity can help you reduce your effective tax rate plus recapture deductions that in previous years were not allowed since your tax bracket was too high.

Details on pages 183-186.

15. More clarification regarding divorcees being able to claim Social Security benefits of their former spouse.

Details on page on page 312

16. 401(k) ROTH Conversions allowed now for almost everyone.

In 2013, almost everyone—even those younger than 59.5 and not retired—could have converted their 401(k) to a 401(k) ROTH as long as employer offers a 401(k) ROTH. In 2014, more employees will have this opportunity since more employers are allowing ROTH contributions.

Details can be found on pages 53-56.

You can have more than one million dollars FDIC insured at one bank.

F or those of you who have your money scattered among different banks for FDIC insurance reasons, did you know that you can have a lot more than $250,000 insured at one bank? What if we told you that you can have over 4 millions dollars insured at one bank? Well, turn the page and learn what few know about FDIC insurance.

1   *You can have more than one million dollars FDIC insured at one bank.*

T he FDIC recognizes that there are different categories of legal ownership such as single account, joint account, certain retirement accounts, etc.

FDIC coverage can increase by using different categories of legal ownership.

As you can see on the opposite page, you can dramatically increase the amount of FDIC coverage if you can use some or most of these accounts. Since we are talking about large amounts of money and about FDIC insurance. It is important that all parties consult with their own advisors, visit the FDIC web site, and call the FDIC at 1-877-ASK-FDIC.

The limits shown on the chart on the next page refer to the total of all deposits that an account holder has in the ownership categories at each FDIC-insured bank. The chart assumes that all FDIC requirements are met and that changes have not been made to FDIC limits.

Hypothetical Example:

George and Hillary, a hypothetical East Coast couple, have 3 children, 3 grandchildren and IRAs as a result of two pension plan distributions. Each has their own separate corporation for speaking engagements, authoring, and consulting. George and Hillary have had $4,750,000 spread out over 25 banks for years and years for FDIC insurance purposes and they are tired of getting 25 different bank statements every month and having to visit 25 different banks every so often. As George too often says, "Hillary, wherever we go, a crowd appears." George and Hillary consulted with their own tax and legal advisors, visited the FDIC web site, and even called the FDIC at 1-877-ASK-FDIC regarding their initial plan as outlined on page 4. What did they do? Simply turn the page to find out how smart they are together.

Scheduled Decrease On 12/31/13
The increase of FDIC from insurance of $100,00 to $250,000 was made permanent on July 21,2012. (Press Release PR-161-2012)

FDIC Deposit Insurance Coverage Limits

Single Accounts (owned by one person)	$250,000 per owner
Joint Accounts (two or more persons)	$250,000 per co-owner
Certain Retirement Accounts (including IRAs)	$250,000 per owner
Revocable Trust Accounts	$250,000 per owner, per beneficiary, up to 5 beneficiaries (more coverage is available with 6 or more beneficiaries*)
Corporation Partnership and Unincorporated Association Accounts	$250,000 per corporation, partnership, or unincorporated association
Irrevocable Trust Accounts	$250,000 for the non-contingent, ascertainable interest of each beneficiary
Employee Benefit Plan Accounts	$250,000 for the non-contingent, ascertainable interest of each plan participant
Government Accounts	$250,000 per official custodian

*Subject to specific limitations and requirements

Source: http://www.FDIC.gov

Bank Merger or Acquisition:
Separate insurance coverage is maintained for 6 months after the merger for customers who have deposits at both institutions. Separate insurance for CD issued by the acquired bank maintained until maturity.

Death of a Beneficiary
No grace period. In most cases the death of beneficiary will immediately reduce the deposit insurance coverage of the owner's deposit account.

Death of Owner
The FDIC insures the deceased owner's accounts as though the owner is still alive for a period of 6 months following his or her death.

1

You can have more than one million dollars FDIC insured at one bank.

Initially, George and Hillary were considering putting $4,750,000 into the following different categories of legal ownership at one FDIC insured bank. They wanted to each put $250,000 into a single account, $250,000 into a joint account, $250,000 from each of their IRAs, and $250,000 from each of their corporate savings. Since they have 3 children and 3 grandchildren whom they love very much, they each wanted to put $250,000 into 6 revocable trust accounts where each account listed a different child or grandchild as beneficiary. They chose a revocable trust account instead of an irrevocable trust account so they could change the beneficiary at any time. As Hillary too often said, "If Ella Rose begins thinking about running off with a motorcycle gang, I can remind her how expensive that decision could be."

What advice did they get from their tax and legal advisors? They were told that they could do what they had planned but to make sure 1) that they should either withdraw the interest often since interest earned on the $250,000 would exceed the $250,000 FDIC limit or they should put less than $250,000 into the CD so the interest and deposit never exceeds the $250,000 FDIC maximum, 2) that they should soul-search to see how important it was for them to terminate the relationships they had with the bank staffs of so many banks, 3) to continue consulting their tax and legal advisors before every important decision, and 4) go to www.fdic.gov and call FDIC since you can never be too careful.

Next Steps

- Visit http://www.fdic.gov and call 1-877-ASK-FDIC.
- Talk to your legal and tax advisors.

secret

FDIC reports that almost 20% of all bank deposits are *not* insured.

In the FDIC's 75 year plus history, no bank customer has ever lost a single penny of "insured deposits" *but* not all deposits are insured. Turn the page to see if your bank deposits are FDIC insured.

2 *FDIC reports that almost 20% of all bank deposits are not insured.*

W hile it is so easy to have all or most of your money insured by the FDIC in a FDIC-insured institution, so many dollars are not insured due to bank depositor's neglect, carelessness, misunderstanding, and in a handful of instances, investor fraud. FDIC reports that almost 20% of all bank deposits are not insured.

What are the most common mistakes?

- Allowing your money to accumulate more than the FDIC limit, currently $250,000.

- Depositing money in separate branches of an FDIC-insured institution is *not* separately insured.

- Keeping too much money in 2 FDIC insured institutions after they are both owned by the same entity.

- Trust accounts in the same FDIC insured institutions that exceed the FDIC limit with the same beneficiary.

What does the FDIC insure at an FDIC insured institution?

- Checking

- NOW accounts

- Money Market Deposit Accounts (MMDA) not to be confused with Money Market Funds

- Time Deposits such as Certificates of Deposit

4 Reasons Why Some CDs Are Not Insured And What Can Be Insured

Common Mistakes

- Allowing CD to be greater than FDIC ceiling

- Having CDs in separate branches

- CDs in 2 banks owned by the same entity

- Trust accounts with same beneficiary

What Does the FDIC Insure?

- Checking
- NOW accounts
- Time deposits and CDs
- Money market deposit accounts
  (Not money market funds)

What is best for you depends upon your circumstances. Turn the page to learn what your next steps could be. This secret is not investment advice, but it is a suggestion that you should think about your retirement savings regularly.

FDIC reports that almost 20% of all bank deposits are not insured.

Next Steps

- Confirm that your deposits are within insurance limits by using the Electronic Deposit Insurance Estimator at http://www.fdic.gov/EDIE or by calling 1-877-ASK-FDIC.

- Confirm that the bank is insured by visiting www.fdic.gov/bankfind.

- Be wary of "too good to be true" interest rates or other "rich promises."

- Consult with your tax and legal advisors.

- Take baby steps and stay diversified so you are less apt to be seriously affected if interest rates, the economy, FDIC legislation, and promises go in the wrong direction.

secret **3**

Laddering CDs gives you liquidity plus protects you from interest rate volatility.

Every day, more CD owners are learning the secret to laddering their CDs in order to get more liquidity and protection from interest rate volatility. If you want to lock in interest rates in case interest rates decrease, plus be in the position to benefit if interest rates increase, turn the page to see how "laddering" 3 CDs over 3 time periods can potentially give your CD portfolio a new dimension.

3 · Laddering CDs gives you liquidity plus protects you from interest rate volatility.

Liquidity every year, or every 30 days, and smoothing out interest rate volatility to some extent is possible with CD laddering. In the example on the opposite page, we illustrate 3 CDs with 3 "ladder rungs," in other words, 3 CDs with 3 term periods of 1-3 years. However, "laddering" can work with shorter or longer term periods and with more than 3 CDs too.

In our hypothetical example, we purchase 3 CDs. The first one matures in 1 year, the second one matures in 2 years, and the third one matures in 3 years. When the first 1 year CD matures at the end of year 1, you can put your initial deposit plus accrued interest from the 1 year CD into a new 3 year CD that will mature in another 3 years. Why 3 years? As you will soon see, we are creating a pattern where every year, one of your CDs matures.

In the second year, the 2 year CD matures and you can put the initial deposit plus accrued interest from the 2 year CD into a new 3 year CD. In the third year, your initial 3 year CD matures and you can again put the initial deposit plus accrued interest from the initial 3 year CD into a new 3 year CD. As you can see from the chart on the opposite page, one of your CDs matures every year.

Do you have to renew a 3 year CD every time? No! When your CDs mature each year, you can do anything you want with the money. You can take off to Tahiti for 2 weeks, reposition the money to another bank paying a higher interest rate, or lock in a highly competitive interest rate for 10 years.

(Continued on page 12)

Laddering CDs Give You Annual Liquidity

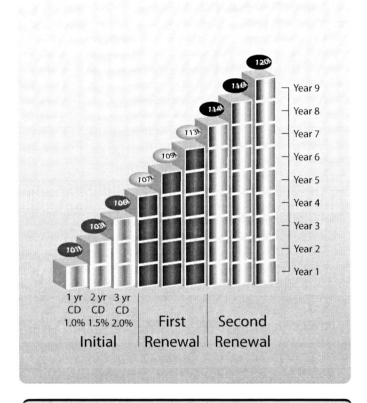

What is best for you depends upon your circumstances. Turn the page to learn what your next steps could be. This secret is not investment advice, but it is a suggestion that you should think about your retirement savings regularly.

3   *Laddering CDs gives you liquidity plus protects you from interest rate volatility.*

(Continued from page 10)

How can this help you with interest rate volatility? If you think that interest rates will not go much lower than they are now, ladder your CDs with 30 day, 60 day and 90 day maturities so you are more apt to benefit from increasing interest rates when your CDs mature. If you feel that interest rates are about to plummet, consider locking in a CD interest rate for 5 years or even 10 years.

If you do not own a crystal ball like most of us and you have no idea where interest rates are going, laddering your CDs among 5 term periods from 1-5 years can be an effective way to protect yourself. If interest rates rise, 40% of your money like your money in the 1 and 2 year CDs will soon get a higher interest rate at maturity. If interest rates plummet, 40% of your money is getting a higher interest rate with the money in the 4 year and 5 year CDs.

Next Steps

- Ask your bank representative or broker:
  1. to show you how you can ladder some of your money with their CDs.

  2. if their CDs are callable. In other words, ask if the bank can terminate the CD before maturity if interest rates become lower. If so, you may not be able to lock in interest rates for 3 to 10 years if the bank can "call" them.

  3. for a printout that will explain their fees for premature withdrawals before maturity.

- Make sure that money becomes due like clockwork like either every year or every 90 or 30 days. Said differently, creating CD maturities of 1, 3, and 5 years can create a gap of time where no money matures.

- Consult with your tax and legal advisors regarding CD and Annuity Laddering.

- If Annuity Laddering is recommended by your tax and legal advisors, reach out to insurance professional to see their examples of Annuity Laddering. Then, circle back to your tax and legal advisors for their final okay.

CD interest rates are far more volatile than you think.

Having some of your money in the bank often makes good sense since it does protect you from risk to principal. However, having all of your money in the bank does not protect you from interest rate risk. Turn the page if you want to see the roller coaster ride of Certificates of Deposit over the past 48 years.

4 *CD interest rates are far more volatile than you think.*

W hile Certificates of Deposit can protect you from risk to principal, they do not protect you from interest rate risk. This is unfortunate since too many retirees rely on their Certificates of Deposit interest as a source of income.

As you can see on the chart on the next page, interest rates for Certificates of Deposit for the past almost 50 years have been unbelievably volatile with interest rates plummeting by as much as 40% from one year to the next. A 40% decrease in income from one year to the next can mean an abrupt change to where you live and how you live.

Does that mean that you should not put your money in the bank? No, having money in the bank is a wise thing to do. But, you should not put all of your money in the bank or in any one financial product.

Fortunately, there are solutions to consider. Firstly, you can get a Certificate of Deposit with a 5 year interest rate guarantee so your interest income can remain the same for 5 years. Naturally, if interest rates rise or decrease elsewhere, your interest rate remains unchanged during this 5 year period.

Secondly, you can "ladder" your Certificates of Deposit so a) income can remain level from one year to the next and b) you can partially benefit from either increasing or decreasing interest rates (see Secret 3 about the advantages and disadvantages to "laddering" CDs).

Thirdly, you can receive a guaranteed stream of income from an insurance company via a Lifetime Income Rider or guaranteed lifetime income using an Immediate Annuity with a Lifetime option.

CD Volatility Since 1965

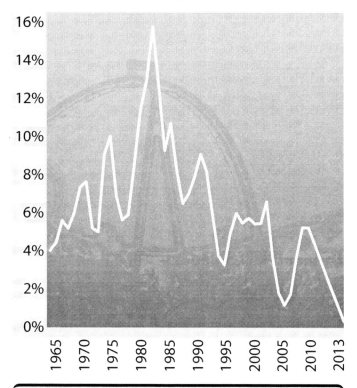

Solution: Diversify among a variety of products that can potentially protect you from risk to losing purchasing power, risk to principal, and interest rate movements.

Source 1: Federal Reserve Statistical Release The rate on certificates of deposit, CDs, is a simple average of dealer rates on negotiable certificates of deposit nationally traded in the secondary market. Rates are determined for each business day.

Source 2: www.bankrate.com; 2013 average 6 month CD on Bankrate.com was 0.41%; 2013 average 5 year CD on Bankrate.com was 1.36%

What is best for you depends upon your circumstances. Turn the page to learn what your next steps could be. This secret is not investment advice, but it is a suggestion that you should think about your retirement savings regularly.

CD interest rates are far more volatile than you think.

Solution to consider:

When planning for retirement, diversify your dollars among a variety of products that can collectively protect you from risk to principal, risk to interest rate movements, and risk to losing purchasing power.

Next Steps

- Keep at least 6 months' income in FDIC insured money market accounts or passbook savings or in slightly higher yielding 30 day CDs.

- Diversify and make sure your account(s) do not exceed FDIC limits by consulting with your tax and legal advisor, banker, and www.fdic.org.

5

A $250,000 CD becomes partially uninsured one day after you own it.

O ur Dads and Moms often reminded us how much less our new car was worth the day we drove our brand new car off of the dealer's lot. However, our Dads and Moms forgot to warn us about FDIC insurance. Turn the page to learn what Dad and Mom should have told you.

5

A $250,000 CD becomes partially uninsured one day after you own it.

When you drove your new Mustang, Dodge Charger, Plymouth Duster, and Edsel off the car lot, it lost 25% or more in value in one split second. When you flipped that Willie Mays or Duke Snyder or Mickey Mantle baseball card in the school playground, it would eventually be worth thousands less because of that "one flip." While you could not have done anything to prevent your assets from plummeting in value back then, you can now avoid having some of your CD dollars only partially FDIC insured.

The basic FDIC insurance amount is $250,000 per depositor per FDIC insured bank per legal ownership.* This $250,000 includes principal and accrued interest. Said differently, every dollar of interest earned and left to accrue on the $250,000 deposit is *not* FDIC insured.

What does this amount to in dollars and cents? Assuming a 3% interest rate on $250,000, there would be $7,500 of accrued interest *not* FDIC insured after one year and $15,000 of accrued interest after two years.

On the opposite page, we have calculated the approximate amount of principal you would need to deposit in order for your CD to be fully FDIC insured using both the current FDIC limit, $250,000, and the FDIC limit scheduled for January 1, 2014, $100,000.

*Please see Secret 1.

What You Need To Deposit To Stay Within FDIC Limits

Today			
Deposit	**Interest**	**Term**	**Maturity**
$238,093	5%	1 yr	$250,000
$195,882	5%	5 yrs	$250,000
$240,385	4%	1 yr	$250,000
$205,482	4%	5 yrs	$250,000
$242,719	3%	1 yr	$250,000
$215,652	3%	5 yrs	$250,000
January 1, 2014			
$95,237	5%	1 yr	$100,000
$78,353	5%	5 yrs	$100,000
$96,154	4%	1 yr	$100,000
$82,193	4%	5 yrs	$100,000
$97,088	3%	1 yr	$100,000
$86,261	3%	5 yrs	$100,000

Values are approximate. Please ask your banker for the exact amount.

What is best for you depends upon your circumstances. Turn the page to learn what your next steps could be. This secret is not investment advice, but it is a suggestion that you should think about your retirement savings regularly.

5 *A $250,000 CD becomes partially uninsured one day after you own it.*

Options to consider:

- Put less than the FDIC insured limit into the CD.

Next Steps

- Consult with your tax and legal advisors.
- Reach out to your banker or your broker.
- Ask for a printout that describes FDIC insurance.
- Visit the website: www.FDIC.org.
- Call FDIC 1-877-ASK-FDIC.

secret **6**

Taxes and inflation can devour all of your interest.

W hile some say that there are only 2 things for certain: Death and Taxes, we add inflation to that list of certainties. And, when inflation is addressed, people are shocked when they see the negative return that taxes and inflation can have on their taxable interest. On the following page, we show an example of what happened to our Moms and Dads in 1950 because of taxes and inflation. In the Resource Section of this book, we show what your Mom and Dad were getting the year you were born.

6   *Taxes and inflation can devour all of your interest.*

O n the opposite page, we show what happened in 1950 to many of our Moms and Dads. Money at the bank was getting 1.22% interest. The lowest tax bracket was 17.4% which means they were only keeping 82.6% of their interest. In other words, Mom and Dad were only keeping 82.6% of the 1.22%, in other words, 1.01%. In our opinion, 1.01% is okay with a zero percent inflation rate. However, inflation in 1950 for Mom and Dad was 1.30 % resulting in a actual return of -0.29%.

In the Resource Section of this book, we give you examples so you can see what your Mom and Dad were really getting the year you were born.

However, the actual return you are getting this year is far more important than when you were born.

Figure out your real return by answering the questions below and then subtracting or multiplying.

Are you happy with that real return? If not, turn the page to learn new steps to take.

1. What interest rate are you receiving on one of your CDs?

2. Now subtract your tax bracket from 100

3. Multiply line 2 times line 1 to get your after tax return

4. What rate of inflation do you think we will average over the next few years?

5. Now subtract the inflation rate (line 4) from your after tax return (line 3) to figure out your real return on your CD

The Real Return That Bank Depositors Got Because Of Taxes And Inflation

Year	⟶	1950
Interest rate	⟶	1.22%
What you keep	⟶	82.60%
After-tax return	⟶	1.01%
Inflation	⟶	1.30%
Actual return	⟶	-0.29%

What is best for you depends upon your circumstances. Turn the page to learn what your next steps could be. This secret is not investment advice, but it is a suggestion that you should think about your retirement savings regularly.

Taxes and inflation can devour all of your interest.

Next Steps

- Consider placing some of your money into a tax-deferred annuity to lessen the negative impact of annual taxes and inflation.

- Consult with your tax and legal advisors.

- Reach out to your insurance or investment professional.

- Remember to keep at least 6 months' income in highly liquid short-term FDIC insured CDs.

- Take cautious baby steps; see how the annuity feels for a year or two before buying annuity #2 .

- Always circle back to your tax and or your legal advisors for their opinion on the product(s) you are about to buy.

secret 7

Attention Heirs: You can easily find out if you inherited any bank money from a relative.

According to the FDIC, they receive hundreds of calls and letters each year from people trying to see if their runaway Dad, Aunt Matilda, or Uncle Buck left them any money in old bank accounts. Sometimes, they get the answer that a bank, state government, or FDIC has these forgotten assets and they're available to claim. Do you have a departed relative who thought you were special? If so, turn the page since "your ship may have come in."

Attention Heirs: You can easily find out if you inherited any bank money from a relative.

While FDIC officials say that, in most cases, there is no treasure waiting because the original owners withdrew the money from their bank account or cleaned out the safe deposit box long ago, FDIC Consumer News offers the following suggestions for getting assets out of the lost-and-not-found department at a bank or a government agency.

If you discover evidence of an old account or safe deposit box, find out if the institution is open or closed. The bank or savings institution may still exist under the same name or under a different name (common after bank mergers), or it may be closed. One way is to search the FDIC's online directory of insured institutions. The FDIC database enables you to trace the history of an institution, even after several mergers.

If the financial institution is still open, ask for a status report on the old accounts. Among the possible outcomes: The original owner closed the account or removed the valuables. The account or safe deposit box may still be at the institution's property office in the state where the owner lived or did business. Or, as a result of years of inactivity, the account became "dormant" and—under state law—the assets were "escheated" (transferred) to the state unclaimed.

A good place to begin your search for assets sent to the state is online by Googling the words "state and unclaimed assets." When you do, you can find resources that can help you. If a state has your funds, and you have proof of ownership, the funds can be released.

Turn the page to learn how to claim money if the bank was closed by the government and how long you have to claim your newly found money.

(Continued on page 28)

FDIC Consumer News

Important Update: Changes in FDIC Deposit Insurance Coverage

The FDIC deposit insurance rules have undergone a series of changes starting in the fall of 2008. As a result, certain previously published information related to FDIC insurance coverage may not reflect the current rules. For details about the recent changes, visit Changes in FDIC Deposit Insurance Coverage. For more information about FDIC insurance, go to www.fdic.gov/deposit/deposits/index.html or call toll-free 1-877-ASK-FDIC (1-877-275-3342). For the hearing-impaired, the number is 1-800-925-4618.

Summer 2011

Lost and Found or Safe and Sound: How to Solve Mysteries of Old Bank Accounts

Have you ever found an old bank statement, passbook, certificate of deposit or receipt for a safe deposit box and wondered if there is "lost" money or other assets waiting for you or a loved one? This is especially a common occurrence for people who serve as an executor of a deceased person's estate or as a financial caregiver for an ill or elderly friend or relative. To help you research old bank accounts and, perhaps,

Source: www.fdic.org

Attention Heirs: You can easily find out if you inherited any bank money from a relative.

(Continued from page 26)

If the bank was closed by the government, find out if the deposits and safe deposit boxes were transferred to another institution or to the FDIC. Start by searching the FDIC database described previously or by calling the FDIC. In most cases, there is an acquiring institution for the failed bank's deposits and safe deposit boxes. If not, the FDIC will mail insurance checks to depositors and send letters to renters of boxes about how and when to remove the contents.

Some people never claim their insured deposit from the FDIC and, under federal law, forfeit the money. Under current rules in effect for failures as of June 1993, people have 18 months from the date of the failure to claim their insured funds from the FDIC. At the end of that period, the FDIC sends any unclaimed deposits to the state unclaimed property office. "The depositor may be able to recover these funds from the state for 10 years," explains FDIC attorney Catherine Ribnick, "but after that time, any money remaining unclaimed is returned to the FDIC's deposit insurance funds and is no longer available to be claimed."

Next Steps

- Visit www.fdic.gov.
- Call FDIC at 1-877-ASK-FDIC.

Source for this secret almost in its entirety http://www.fdic.gov/consumers/ consumer/news/cnspr02/lost.html.

You can lose some of your bank deposit if you withdraw your money too soon.

W hile it was no surprise to us that penalties for withdrawing your principal from your CD too soon could result in losing some of the original deposit, we were shocked to learn that the early withdrawal penalties can vary from bank to bank. Turn the page to see how high and how low bank penalties can be.

8

You can lose some of your bank deposit if you withdraw your money too soon.

For all the years we owned CDs, we incorrectly assumed that bank penalties were all the same and that the penalties were probably regulated by the FDIC. In fact, during the first draft of this book, we reached out to one of our banks for their penalty fee schedule for each CD maturity from 30 days to 5 years. In an attempt to assure accuracy, we circled back to the same bank months later for reconfirmation. It was then when they proudly announced that their penalty fee schedule had changed for new CD purchases.

After more research, we found that 1) banks decide what their early withdrawal penalties are, 2) many banks—but not all banks—have a similar early withdrawal penalty as seen on the opposite page, and 3) it is possible to buy a CD with NO early withdrawal fees.

Early withdrawal penalties for depositors withdrawing their principal prior to CD maturity are usually expressed in "days loss of interest"' with many banks. As you see on the opposite page, the penalty increases from 90 days loss of interest to one year loss of interest as the maturity period increases. And, since the penalty is calculated in days loss of interest, the higher the interest rate, the higher the penalty.

Naturally, it makes sense for a bank or for an insurance company to have early withdrawal penalties. As we have asked on many occasions, "Do you want your money to be with an institution that is trying to protect itself from a "run on the bank" or do you want your money with an institution that is not trying to protect itself from a "run on the bank?"

What is "a run on the bank?" For those of you who have seen the movie *It's A Wonderful Life* with Jimmy Stewart and Donna Reed, the newly married couple saw an unusually long line of depositors outside the Bailey Savings and Loan. When George, played by Jimmy Stewart, inquired what was wrong, he discovered that they all wanted their money right away.

(Continued on page 32)

Bank Penalties For Premature Withdrawals From CDs

Interest rates for CD maturing:	
less than 1 year*	**Penalty**
2%	$500
4%	$1,000
6%	$1,500
8%	$2,000
10%	$2,500

1-3 years**	**Penalty**
2%	$1,000
4%	$2,000
6%	$3,000
8%	$4,000
10%	$5,000

longer than 3 years***	**Penalty**
2%	$2,000
4%	$4,000
6%	$6,000
8%	$8,000
10%	$10,000

Assumes a $100,000 CD.
*90 days loss of interest with possible loss of principal.
**180 days loss of interest with possible loss of principal.
***1 year loss of interest with possible loss of principal.

What is best for you depends upon your circumstances. Turn the page to learn what your next steps could be. This secret is not investment advice, but it is a suggestion that you should think about your retirement savings regularly.

8

You can lose some of your bank deposit if you withdraw your money too soon.

(Continued from page 30)

That is a "run on the bank" and as George explained to the angry nervous crowd, he did not have their money since their money had been loaned to their neighbors, neighbors who were in the same line with them.

Fortunately, things have changed. We now have FDIC insurance up to a certain level. However, what has not changed is how dangerous it can be for an institution to have more withdrawal requests than new deposits especially in an increasing interest rate environment.

Said differently, early withdrawal penalties are both a form of protection for the institution and potential protection for you too since there can be advantages to you if your institution remains solvent.

Most banks do 1) not impose early withdrawal penalties on interest withdrawn, 2) subtract penalties from the deposit even if this results in you getting back less than your CD deposit, and 3) waive early withdrawal penalties if the CD owner dies. Should you be alarmed? No! However, you should follow the Next Steps.

Next Steps

- Ask your banker to explain the penalties and ask for their penalty fee disclosure brochure.

- Go online and research which banks have lower penalty fees; see Short Bonus Secret 4 at the end of the book for online CD shopping web sites.

- Keep at least 6 months' income either in low yielding penalty-free accounts like FDIC insured money market accounts or passbook savings or in slightly higher yield 30 day CDs.

- Diversify and make sure your account(s) does not exceed FDIC limits by consulting with your tax and legal advisor, banker, and www.fdic.org.

- Re-read Secrets 1 and 2 and show them to your advisors and bankers for their comments.

secret 9

How my Uncle Donald* started with a penny and became filthy rich.

While this may not be a secret, it is a shocking revelation. Shocking since it illustrates the power of saving regularly. In fact, all you need is a 0% return, no losses, saving 1 penny on the first day, and simply doubling it every day thereafter. In other words, you will save 2 pennies in day two, 4 pennies in day three and 8 pennies in day four, etc. At the end of 30 days, you will have saved over 10 million dollars. Impossible? Just turn the page to be a believer in saving regularly.

*In his dreams.

How my Uncle Donald started with a penny and became filthy rich.

The power of saving is illustrated on the opposite page where we show the hypothetical example of someone saving more money each day. Do we expect you to do this? Heck, no! Do we expect you to see the importance of saving and that double digit interest rates or returns are "not" needed to accumulate wealth? Absolutely, yes.

On the opposite page, we assume a hypothetical couple saving 1 penny on the first day and "just" doubling it every day for 30 days at a zero percent return. As you can see, after 30 short days, they will have accumulated over 10 million dollars.

Admittedly, we recognize no one can do what is proposed here. However, if we can show you the importance of saving now instead of later and that you do not need extraordinary annual returns to accumulate wealth, then this secret might change your life.

Bottom line: Begin saving today! Why? It is your life!

A 30-Day Savings Program Goes From 1 Penny In Day One, 2 Pennies In Day Two, 4 Pennies In Day Three, Etc.

Day	Amount Saved	Balance	Day	Amount Saved	Balance
1	$0.01	$0.01	16	$328	$655
2	$0.02	$0.03	17	$655	$1,311
3	$0.04	$0.07	18	$1,311	$2,621
4	$0.08	$0.15	19	$2,621	$5,243
5	$0.16	$0.31	20	$5,243	$10,486
6	$0.32	$0.63	21	$10,486	$20,972
7	$0.64	$1.27	22	$20,972	$41,943
8	$1.28	$2.55	23	$41,943	$83,886
9	$2.56	$5.11	24	$83,886	$167,772
10	$5.12	$10.23	25	$167,772	$335,544
11	$10.24	$20.47	26	$335,544	$671,089
12	$20.48	$40.95	27	$671,089	$1,342,177
13	$40.96	$81.91	28	$1,342,177	$2,684,355
14	$81.92	$163.83	29	$2,684,355	$5,368,709
15	$163.84	$327.67	30	$5,368,709	$10,737,418

The above chart assumes a 30-day savings program with NO interest or return. The savings program starts off with you saving 1 cent in day one and then simply doubling what you save each day, in other words, saving 1 cent in day one, 2 cents in day two, 4 cents in day three, etc.

The column titled "Balance" shows how much money would have accumulated had you saved at this unrealistic rate for only 30 days. The sole purpose of this chart is to show the power of saving regularly and that wealth can be created even at a 0% return.

How my Uncle Donald started with a penny and became filthy rich.

Next Steps

- Consult with your tax and legal advisors.

- Reach out to your insurance professional regarding products that can help you save.

- Circle back to your tax and legal advisors regarding the products that you are considering buying.

- Take cautious baby steps, but act if it is in your best interest.

- Diversify.

- Read what you are about to sign.

You are more likely to live longer than you think.

T he life expectancy of a newly born baby in 1950 was 65.6. Today, the life expectancy for a newly born baby is closer to age 78. And, everyday life expectancy increases. So much so that respected medical experts are now projecting life expectancies beyond any one's expectations. In fact, according to the medical journal, *The Lancet*, more than 50% of babies born today will live to age 100 and older. To learn the age that you might reach, breathe in, and turn the page.

10 *You are more likely to live longer than you think.*

The estimates on the opposite page come from some of the most respected names and brightest minds in America.

I am going to sound arrogant unless you read the next two sentences slowly:

> "I have a great deal of money if I die soon. But, I may not have enough money saved if Mrs. H or I live to age 94 and there is a 50% plus actuarial chance of that happening."

Plus, if inflation averages 4% plus like it has since 1973-2012 and if interest rates remain low, I know for a fact that I do not have enough money.

Will you have enough saved? You can, if you read this entire book.

Facts About Aging

a. There are 51,000 people age 100 and older in the United States.

b. In the year 2030, there are projections that there will be 324,000 people age 100 and older (almost a 1,000% increase since 1990).

c. Hallmark, the greeting card company, says that by the end of the decade, they expect to sell more than 70,000 centenarian birthday cards each year.

d. 70 million people in the United States will be 65 and older in 2035. This number is more than twice the current population of Canada.

e. Today, people age 50 and older now control 80% of the money in the U.S. Savings and Loan institutions and represent $66.00 of every $100.00 invested in the stock market.

f. The average 21st Century American will spend more years caring for their parents than for their children.

g. In 2080, the average life expectancy in the U.S. will be 100 for men and 103 for women.

Sources: (a) 2000 U.S. Census Bureau, (b) Augusta Chronicle, (c) Living To Age 100, T. Perls, M. Silver, and J. Lauerman, (d) Age Wave, K. Dychtwald and U.S. Census Bureau, (e) Age Power, K. Dychtwald, (f) Age Power, K. Dychtwald, National Association of Area Agencies on Aging, 1998-99 National Directory for Eldercare Information and Referral (Washington, DC. NAAA, 1999), (g) Dare To Be 100, W. Bortz II, M.D., International Journal of Forecasting, K. Manton, Duke University.

What is best for you depends upon your circumstances. Turn the page to learn what your next steps could be. This secret is not investment advice, but it is a suggestion that you should think about your retirement savings regularly.

You are more likely to live longer than you think.

Next Steps

- Pay yourself first every month (see Secret 27).

- Think about your money on a regular basis (see Secret 34).

- Surround yourself with financial mentors (see Secret 31).

- Look at annuitizing some of your annuities for lifetime income and talk to your tax and legal advisors and insurance professionals about the merits of some of the Lifetime Income Benefit riders that some Fixed and Variable Annuities now have (see Secret 65 and 68).

The Social Security system will probably change.

In 1945, there were 41.9 workers paying in for one Social Security recipient. Today, there are only 2.8 workers paying in for one Social Security recipient. In 1935, when Social Security was enacted, the average man lived to age 62 so a retirement age of 65 made all the sense in the world. Simply turn the page to learn how Social Security might change.

11 *The Social Security system will probably change.*

While some might feel that it would be unwise to dramatically change Social Security benefits, it might be more harmful to allow Social Security to continue going in the direction that it currently is. As you will see in the chart on the following page, in 1945, there were 41.9 workers paying into the Social Security system for every one retiree. In 1950, only 16.5 workers. In 1975, 3.7. In 1990, 3.4 workers. Today, there are only 2.8 workers paying into the Social Security system for every one retiree. By 2033, there will be 2.1 workers for each beneficiary.

When Social Security was enacted, life expectancy was 62 so a retirement age of 65 perhaps made sense back then. But, life expectancy is now 75.8 years for a male and 81.7 for a female. And, since life expectancy is no longer 62 like it was in the 1930s, should we still be holding on to age 65, an age that was selected over 70 years ago?

In the opinion of some, Social Security benefits must decline or start later. In the opinion of most, the quality of our retirement should not be contingent upon Social Security or help from our family. Solutions to consider, when planning for retirement, take advantage of qualified and non-qualified retirement plans, just in case.

Facts

• In 2013, over 58 million Americans will receive $816 billion in Social Security benefits.

• In 2012, the average monthly benefit for a retired worker was $1,269; $1,221 for a survivor.

• Social Security benefits represent 39% of the income for the elderly.

• 23% of married couples and 46% of unmarried persons rely on Social Security for 90% or more of their retirement income.

Source: www.socialsecurtiy.gov

How Many Workers Are Paying Into The Social Security System For Every One Beneficiary

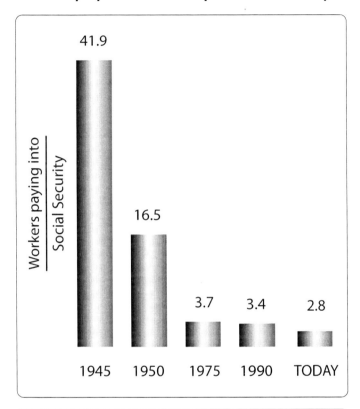

Workers paying into / Social Security

41.9	16.5	3.7	3.4	2.8
1945	1950	1975	1990	TODAY

Solution: Take advantage of non-qualified and qualified retirement plans to supplement Social Security benefits, just in case.

What is best for you depends upon your circumstances. Turn the page to learn what your next steps could be. This secret is not investment advice, but it is a suggestion that you should think about your retirement savings regularly.

The Social Security system will probably change.

Next Steps

- Consult with your tax and legal advisors.
- Based upon the recommendation of your advisor, reach out to your insurance professional.
- Action begins with a decision.
- Take baby steps.
- Diversify.

secret

It might be smarter for some to get the smaller Social Security benefit at age 62.

Approximately 50% of people select the "reduced" Social Security benefit at age 62 rather than wait until 66 or until age 70 to get higher benefits. Some of those people made the right decision. Unfortunately, some did not. Marital status, spousal lifetime earnings, savings, health, and, naturally, income coming in are factors that you and your tax and legal advisors must consider before making this important decision.

12   *It might be smarter for some to get the smaller Social Security benefit at age 62.*

You are eligible for Social Security anytime from 62 to age 70. For those born between 1943 and 1954, the full retirement age is 66. As a result, you can begin receiving "reduced benefits" at age 62 or "full benefits" at age 66 or "enhanced benefits" at age 70.

While your lifetime earnings will control what your benefit is, one example might be:

> Age 62 - $750 a month
> Age 66 - $1000 a month
> Age 70 - $1320 a month

On the opposite page, we illustrate the difference between taking the "reduced" benefit to the "enhanced" benefit. As you can see, assuming that you do have other income coming in between ages 62 and 70 and that you do live to age 80, the "enhanced" is clearly more beneficial to you and your surviving spouse.

What should you do? While you and your advisors can only make that decision since your circumstances may be different from others, we have listed some of the topics that your advisors will want to discuss with you.

Marital status
Generally speaking, men make more money than women during their lifetimes and men are more apt to predecease their spouse as well. The disadvantage of "men" taking the "reduced" benefit is that surviving spouse will get the "reduced" benefit after he dies.

Savings
If you have little savings and little income coming in, your advisors might say that getting $750 a month from Social Security is a lot better than borrowing $750 a month at double digit interest rates.

If you have savings, consider the alternate on page 319.

The Difference Between Starting Social Security at Ages 62 and 70

Age	Mthly Pmts	Cumulative Amount	Mthly Pmts	Cumulative Amount
62-69	$750	$72,000	n/a	n/a
70	$750	$81,000	$1,320	$15,840
71	$750	$90,000	$1,320	$31,680
72	$750	$99,000	$1,320	$47,520
73	$750	$108,000	$1,320	$63,360
74	$750	$117,000	$1,320	$79,200
75	$750	$126,000	$1,320	$95,040
76	$750	$135,000	$1,320	$110,880
77	$750	$144,000	$1,320	$126,720
78	$750	$153,000	$1,320	$142,560
79	$750	$162,000	$1,320	$158,400
80	$750	$171,000	$1,320	$174,240
81	$750	$180,000	$1,320	$190,080
82	$750	$189,000	$1,320	$205,920
83	$750	$198,000	$1,320	$221,760
84	$750	$207,000	$1,320	$237,600
85	$750	$216,000	$1,320	$253,440
86	$750	$225,000	$1,320	$269,280
87	$750	$234,000	$1,320	$285,120
88	$750	$243,000	$1,320	$300,960
89	$750	$252,000	$1,320	$316,800
90	$750	$261,000	$1,320	$332,640

Sources: http://www.SSA.gov/pubs/10147.html; W.V.H., Inc.

What is best for you depends upon your circumstances. Turn the page to learn what your next steps could be. This secret is not investment advice, but it is a suggestion that you should think about your retirement savings regularly.

Please see page 319 for alternatives.

12 *It might be smarter for some to get the smaller Social Security benefit at age 62.*

Health

If your health and your spouse's health is not up to par and if your family history also reflects shorter life expectancies, your advisors might say that getting the "reduced" benefit is better than not getting any benefit at all.

Income Coming In

You can still work and receive "reduced" and "full" benefits. If you are younger than full retirement age and if your earnings exceed certain dollar amounts, some of your benefit payments during the year will be withheld. This does not mean that you must try to limit your earnings. If Social Security withholds some of your benefits because you continue to work, they will pay you a higher monthly benefit amount when you reach your full retirement age. In other words, if you would like to work and earn more than the exempt amount, you should know that it will not, on average, reduce the total value of lifetime benefits you receive from Social Security. It might actually increase them. (Source: Social Security Administration)

Additional Resources:

From the Social Security Administration:

You can estimate benefit amounts and find more information to help you decide when to start receiving retirement benefits by visiting www.socialsecurity.gov/planners. When you're ready to apply for benefits, you also can apply online at www.socialsecurity.gov/applyforbenefits. Many people can continue to work and still receive retirement benefits. If you want more information on how earnings affect your retirement benefits, ask for How Work Affects Your Benefits (Publication No. 05-10069), which has current annual and monthly earnings limits.

A wealth of other information—including copies of publications—are available on the website at www.socialsecurity.gov. You also can call the toll-free number, 1-800-772-1213. They can answer specific questions from 7 a.m. to 7 p.m., Monday through Friday, and can provide information by automated phone service 24 hours a day.

Next Steps

• Consult with your tax and legal advisor.

secret

You will probably be in a higher tax bracket during retirement.

More people are retiring later, returning to work after retirement, starting a second career, or working part time. However, those are not the only reasons why you will probably be in a higher tax bracket. The U.S. Government's unprecedented debt points to higher income taxes for all of us. How high can income taxes go? If you look at the IRS chart on the next page, you will see that a 70% tax bracket was not too many years ago.

13 *You will probably be in a higher tax bracket during retirement.*

n fact, a new breed of young entrepreneurs age 65 and older are beginning new careers because of financial necessity or to fulfill a lifelong dream of having and owning their own business. Even if income taxes do not rise again, there will be fewer people age 65 and older in the low 15% tax bracket.

However, income taxes will probably rise again via increased tax brackets or modified deductions. The U.S. Government's unprecedented debt coupled with a need to reduce the debt will lead us to higher income taxes and changes for all of us. How high can income taxes go? If you look at the chart on the opposite page, you will see how often and how quickly tax brackets have changed. In fact, you will see that the highest tax bracket was 92% in 1952 for taxable incomes over $400,000 and as high as 50% in 1986 for taxable incomes in excess of $172,250.

Solutions to Consider:

- Accumulate more money tax deferred so you have more left over after taxes.

- Turn to tax-deferred products when tax brackets are increasing.

You Will Probably Be In A Higher Tax Bracket After Retirement

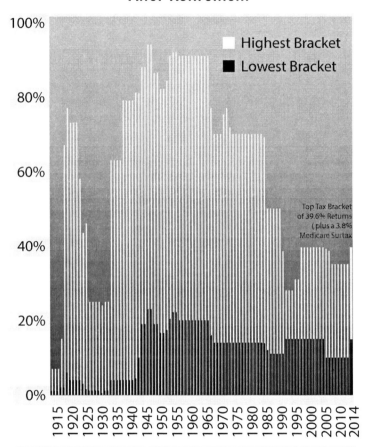

Highest Bracket
Lowest Bracket

Top Tax Bracket
of 39.6% Returns
(plus a 3.8%
Medicare Surtax

Source: Internal Revenue Service

Tax rates shown are for the "regular" income tax applicable to US Citizens and residents

What is best for you depends upon your circumstances. Turn the page to learn what your next steps could be. This secret is not investment advice, but it is a suggestion that you should think about your retirement savings regularly.

You will probably be in a higher tax bracket during retirement.

Next Steps
- Consult with your tax and legal advisors.
- If they feel it's appropriate, reach out to your insurance professional for tax-deferred alternatives.

Converting your 401(k) or IRA to a ROTH could be a big mistake or the best thing you ever do.

Beginning in 2013 and continuing in 2014, many who have a 401(k)—regardless of age, income, etc.— can convert their 401(k) to a ROTH 401(k). In 2010, IRA owners were given this opportunity to convert to ROTH IRAs. However, is it an opportunity for you or an opportunity for the IRS to collect much needed tax revenue when the government needs it the most? Fortunately, it can be an opportunity for you and the government if you know how to make a smart decision. All you have to do is turn the page.

14 *Converting your 401(k) or IRA to a ROTH could be a big mistake or the best thing you ever do.*

W hile the ROTH is an opportunity to withdraw money in the future income tax free, you do have to pay income taxes now. Is it in your best interest to convert your 401(k) to a ROTH 401(k) or your IRA to a ROTH IRA? Please review the following with your tax and legal advisors.

3.8% Medicare Surtax
In 2013, a brand new 3.8% Medicare surtax went into effect for those whose Modified Adjusted Gross Income exceed $250,000 (if married) and $200,000 (single). A ROTH conversion could result in a 3.8% surtax, hence, increasing the real cost of your ROTH conversion.

Your Current and Future Tax Brackets
In the year of the conversion, will your tax bracket be higher or lower than your projected tax bracket during retirement? Your tax and legal advisors might begin leaning toward a ROTH Conversion if they feel that your future tax bracket will be higher than your present tax bracket.

Your Health/Your Heirs
Paying the ROTH Conversion tax and converting taxable income to tax-free income might not be as beneficial if your life expectancy is not what it should be, there is no spouse, and leaving a tax-free legacy to your heirs is a low priority. Your tax and legal advisors might lean toward a ROTH Conversion if you are more apt to live up to life expectancy tables, there is a spouse, and you have adorable and appreciative adult children and grandchildren.

(Continued on page 56)

5 Things To Discuss With Your Tax Advisor

- 3.8% Medicare Surtax

- Your tax bracket now

- Your tax bracket later

- Your health

- Your heirs

- How you pay the conversion tax

What is best for you depends upon your circumstances. Turn the page to learn what your next steps could be. This secret is not investment advice, but it is a suggestion that you should think about your retirement savings regularly.

14 *Converting your 401(k) or IRA to a ROTH could be a big mistake or the best thing you ever do.*

(Continued from page 54)

How will you pay the Conversion Tax

In 2010, tax law allowed those who converted their IRA to a ROTH IRA to defer taxes and spread their income over 2 years, 2011 and 2012. That is no longer the case for IRA owners and this convenience is certainly not available to 401(k) owners. In fact, the genesis of giving 401(k) owners the opportunity to convert was for the government to collect taxes as soon as possible.

Preferred way to pay conversion tax

Will you pay the Conversion Tax from money in your IRA or 401(k) or from money outside your Qualified Plans? Since you could be dramatically reducing the value of your retirement account by paying the conversion tax from your IRA or 401(k) retirement account, your tax and legal advisors might lean in the direction of a ROTH Conversion if you plan to pay the Conversion Tax from dollars outside of your Qualified Plans.

Next Steps

- Consult with your tax and legal advisors; especially since this important piece of legislation titled The American Taxpayer Relief Act is less than 8 days old as of January 10th, 2013.

- See if your employer offers ROTH 401(k)s; currently less than 50% of large corporations do but that will probably increase appreciably.

- If they feel it's appropriate, reach out to your insurance professional for some of the best places to put your ROTH money.

- Circle back with your tax and legal advisors regarding any product that you are about to purchase.

- Diversify.

- Take cautious baby steps.

- IMPORTANT NOTE: IRA conversions to ROTH IRAs can be "undone" (recharacterized). 401(k) conversions to ROTH 401(k)s cannot be "undone" (recharacterized). Please see pages 155-158 regarding recharacterization.

The wrong Consumer Price Index is being used for some Social Security recipients.

T he Consumer Price Indexes, (CPI-U and CPI-W), are the 2 most popular ways to measure inflation. However, the CPI-U and CPI-W may not be the most accurate way to measure the real impact that increasing prices are having on "your" life. If you are wondering how indexes that measure inflation show low rates of inflation when the costs for your medical care, prescription drugs, and insurance are skyrocketing, just turn the page.

15

The wrong Consumer Price Index is being used for some Social Security recipients.

The Consumer Price Index (CPI) is a measure of the average change over time in the prices paid by consumers for a market basket of consumer goods and services. The CPI indexes most commonly used for measuring inflation are:

1. CPI for All Urban Consumers (CPI-U)
2. CPI for Urban Wage Earners and Clerical Workers (CPI-W)

The organization responsible for the Consumer Price Indexes, The Bureau of Labor Statistics, admits, "The CPI-U or CPI-W may not be applicable to all population groups. For example, the CPI-U is designed to measure inflation for the U.S. urban population and thus may not accurately reflect the experience of people living in rural areas." The Bureau of Labor Statistics then unveils on their web site:

"The CPI does not produce official estimates for the rate of inflation experienced by subgroups of the population, such as the "elderly" or the poor. BLS does produce and release an experimental index for the elderly population; however, because of the significant limitations of this experimental index, it should be interpreted with caution."

Friends, we dug deeper and discovered that the "experimental index" that tracks the rate of inflation for those 62 and older has a name. It is called the CPI-E. And, guess what! This experimental index has been around since 1983 and the CPI-E weights the index based on how 62 year old plus people are more apt to spend their money. For example, the CPI-E weights medical care and medical care commodities more heavily than the CPI-U or CPI-W. So while medical care, insurance, and prescription drugs are increasing at an alarming rate, the CPI-E will accurately reflect a higher rate of inflation for those who spend more money on medical care. In an earlier draft of this secret, we had asked, "Do you want

(Continued on page 60)

Which Index Do You Wish Social Security Followed?

Year	CPI-E	CPI-W	CPI-U
1987	4.5	4.5	4.4
1988	4.5	4.4	4.4
1989	5.2	4.5	4.6
1990	6.6	6.1	6.1
1991	3.4	2.8	3.1
1992	3.0	2.9	2.9
1993	3.1	2.5	2.7
1994	2.7	2.7	2.7
1995	2.8	2.5	2.5
1996	3.4	3.3	3.3
1997	1.8	1.5	1.7
1998	1.9	1.6	1.6
1999	2.8	2.7	2.7
2000	3.6	3.4	3.4
2001	1.9	1.3	1.6
2002	2.6	2.4	2.4
2003	2.1	1.6	1.9
2004	3.4	3.4	3.3
2005	3.6	3.5	3.4
2006	2.7	2.4	2.5
2007	4.0	4.3	4.1
2008	0.5	0.5	0.1
2009	2.2	3.4	2.7
2010	1.4	1.7	1.5
2011	2.8	3.2	3
2012	2	2	2
2013	1.6	1.5	1.5

Source: Bureau of Labor Statistics

What is best for you depends upon your circumstances. Turn the page to learn what your next steps could be. This secret is not investment advice, but it is a suggestion that you should think about your retirement savings regularly.

15 *The wrong Consumer Price Index is being used for some Social Security recipients.*

(Continued from page 58)

increases in your retirement benefits to be based on how a younger generation experiences life or on what you purchase? Said differently, do you feel comfortable with your Social Security, military, or civil retirement checks being based on the buying habits of younger people who are less apt to feel the pain when the cost of medical care, prescription drugs, and medical insurance increase annually?"

We now strike the above statement since the CPI-E appears to be in the best interest of almost every generation. On the previous page, we show the difference between the 3 indexes from 1987 to 2012. In those years, the CPI-U and CPI-W had a higher inflation rate than the CPI-E in only 4 years. In all other years, the CPI-E was higher or equal.

Is This Another Conspiracy Theory?

No, we are "not" saying that the government is trying to keep the inflation index low so that increases in Social Security, military, and civil retirement benefits are less. On their web site, www.bls.gov, Bureau of Labor Statistics does an excellent job explaining why the CPI-E is an experimental index and why it has limitations. However, the same web site reports:

"Hobijn and Lagakos (2003) estimated that switching to the CPI-E for cost-of-living increases (COLAs) would move projected insolvency sooner by 3–5 years," and "A projection by SSA's Office of the Chief Actuary estimated that annual COLAs based on the Chained C-CPI-U beginning in 2006 would delay the date of OASDI insolvency by 4 years."

There are 56 million Social Security beneficiaries and 4.1 million military and civil retirees and survivors who are more apt to agree that there could be a better way to measure inflation based on what they purchase.

How Is Each Index Weighted?

Which Index More Accurately Reflects Your Spending Habits?

Expenditure categories	CPI-U	CPI-W	CPI-E
All Items	100.00	100.00	100.00
Food and beverages	15.26	15.80	13.11
Housing	41.02	39.85	45.47
Owners' equivalent rent	23.96	20.81	27.54
Apparel	3.56	3.6	2.46
Transportation	16.90	19.03	14.84
Medical care	7.06	5.67	11.60
Recreation	6.04	5.6	5.43
Education and communications	6.97	6.80	3.81
Other goods and services	3.38	3.52	3.26

Source: Bureau of Labor Statistics
CPI-U = Consumer Price Index for U.S. City Average
CPI-W = Consumer Price Index for U.S. City Average
CPI-E = Consumer Price Index for the Elderly

2009-2010 weights relative importance of components in the Consumer Price Indexes: U.S. city average, December, 2011. Note: The relative importances for the U.S. city average were reissued on March 7, 2012

The wrong Consumer Price Index is being used for some Social Security recipients.

Next Steps

- While some authors would use this topic to urge everyone to write letters to their congressional representative, we would like to go in a different direction.

- Let's stop depending upon the government to use the correct index to measure and influence how we live, where we live, with whom we live.

- We must begin to control our own destiny and almost every secret in this book can be your next step and your children's next step to financial and emotional independence.

secret **16**

Your $100,000 CD could double in value in....

262 short years! With interest rates at historic lows, millions of owners of Certificates of Deposit (CDs) are beginning to rethink how they save or invest for retirement. A CD owner in a 33% tax bracket will see their $100,000 Jumbo CD earning .41% interest double to $200,000 in 262 years after taxes. If you want to see how that compares to past decades, just turn the page slowly. If you want your money to potentially accumulate faster, turn the page as fast as you can.

Your $100,000 CD could double in value in....

Many of us have watched our grandparents and parents rely on bank products. As a result, many of us continue to rely on bank products. However, times may have changed and consumers—more than ever before—are looking for other alternatives. However, the alternatives should be for "some of your money". Regardless of how low interest rates are now for bank products, most bank products are safe. In other words, a 1% return is better than a 10% loss.

However, many consumers today are NOW getting a slightly higher interest rate with NO losses with certain types of annuities. Before we discuss which types of annuities, let's discuss another benefit to CDs.

Historically, bank products have been fast to react during increasing interest rate environments. Said differently, a bank is likely to pay higher interest rates at CD renewals when and if interest rates increase. So if your crystal ball says that interest rates are about to skyrocket during the next year, you might be better off sticking with your .41% interest 6 month CD since you are about to get a pay raise, higher interest rates at renewal.

However, if you do NOT have a crystal ball, doesn't it make sense to get a Multi-Year Guarantee Annuity guaranteeing 1% or more for 3-5 years for some of your bank money? However, in order to get a higher return, tax deferral, and the choice to elect lifetime income, there are surrender charges if you take an excess withdrawal or surrender before the end of the guarantee period; and some Multi-Year Guarantee Annuities have a Market Value Adjustment which is an added surrender penalty if you want to withdraw money during an increasing interest rate environment. But, CDs also have withdrawal penalties since withdrawal penalties protect banks and insurers from a run on the bank.

As you will see on the chart on the opposite page, in 1980, it took 8.3 years for a CD to double after taxes; in 1990, 13.16 years; in 2000 16.29 years. Today, it might take 262 years. A solution to consider? Consider a Multi-Year Guarantee Annuity and turn the page for your Next Steps.

Year	6 Month CD % Rate	Years Money to Double (Before Taxes)	Years Money to Double (After Taxes)
1980	12.94	5.66	8.3
1981	15.79	4.56	6.8
1982	12.57	5.73	8.55
1983	9.28	7.76	11.58
1984	10.71	6.72	10.03
1985	8.24	8.74	13.04
1986	6.50	11.08	16.51
1987	7.01	10.27	15.32
1988	7.91	9.10	13.58
1989	9.08	7.93	11.84
1990	8.17	8.8	13.16
1991	5.91	12.18	18.18
1992	3.76	19.15	28.57
1993	3.28	21.95	32.73
1994	4.96	14.52	21.69
1995	5.98	12.04	17.96
1996	5.47	13.16	19.67
1997	5.73	12.57	18.75
1998	5.44	13.24	19.78
1999	5.46	13.19	19.67
2000	6.59	10.93	16.29
2001	3.66	19.67	29.39
2002	1.81	39.78	59.50
2003	1.17	61.54	92.31
2004	1.74	41.38	61.54
2005	3.73	19.30	28.80
2006	5.24	13.74	20.51
2007	5.23	13.41	20.51
2008	3.14	22.93	34.29
2009	0.87	82.75	124.14
2010	0.63	114	171
2011	0.46	156	232
2012	0.42	171	256
2013	0.41	176	262

What is best for you depends upon your circumstances. Turn the page to learn what your next steps could be. This secret is not investment advice, but it is a suggestion that you should think about your retirement savings regularly. Naturally, CD interests rates only remain level during the maturity period and then renew at a higher or lower interest rate.

All parties should see the insurer disclosure and annuity contract for guaranteed interest rates and values. Bank CDs are insured up to applicable limits by the FDIC. Annuities are insurance products and are NOT insured by the FDIC or any other federal government agency. The guarantees in an annuity contract are subject to the claims-paying ability of the insurer making the guarantees. Annuities have earnings which are taxable upon withdrawal and, if taken before age 59.5, may be subject to IRS penalties. Withdrawals taken during the Surrender Charge period above the penalty-free amount will be subject to Surrender Charges and a possible Market Value Adjustment. Source: Federal Reserve Statistical Release H15; W.V.H., Inc; www.bankrate.com

*Assumes 6-month CD in the secondary market a 33% combined federal and state income tax bracket and interest rates being level.

16 *Your $100,000 CD could double in value in....*

Next Steps

- Consult with your tax and legal advisors.
- Based upon their recommendation, reach out to your insurance professional.
- Action begins with a decision.
- Take cautious baby steps.
- Diversify.

secret

Your neighbors are getting a 50%-like annual return without risk. You can too.

I f you employer promised to match 50 cents for every $1.00 you saved in your 401(k) plan, wouldn't that be almost like a 50% return? According to the Employee Benefit Research Institute, 33% of workers participate in a 401(k) plan. While not all employers match, the typical matching rate among employers is 50 cents on the dollar up to 6% of pay. Sadly, not enough employees take advantage of this employee benefit. Turn the page to learn more.

Source: Employee Benefit Research Institute

Your neighbors are getting a 50%-like annual return without risk. You can too.

On the opposite page, we show the accumulation power of monthly contributions going into a 401(k) plan earning an hypothetical return of 4% and 8%. As you can see, even if your employer does not add more money to your contribution by "matching" it, the tax benefits of you deferring your wages and the tax benefit of your deferred wages potentially accumulating tax deferred could be called the 8th wonder of the world.

The 9th wonder of the world would be if your employer matches the contribution since the accumulation values are up to 60% greater with an employer match since more money is being saved.

Can it get any better? Yes, the chart assumes an employer match of 50 cents on the dollar up to 3% of salary. The typical match is up to 6% of salary. Plus, you can put your 401(k) contribution in a wide variety of accounts with varying degrees of risk from none, low, moderate, to high.

What else should you know about the 9th wonder of the world? If you leave your employer, you can take your contributions, but you cannot take the employer contribution with you unless you stayed with them for a short number of years. This is called *vesting*.

Should you know anything else? Yes, please consider following the Next Steps on the next page.

How Much More Money Could You Have If You Saved More And Your Employer Matched Your Contribution?

Monthly Contributions	Yr	Without Matching		With Matching	
		4%	8%	4%	8%
$300	10	$203,290	$253,412	$270,955	$337,760
	20	$506,364	$815,895	$674,906	$1,087,464
$1,000	10	$147,740	$184,166	$221,610	$276,249
	20	$367,997	$592,947	$551,996	$889,421
$1,376	10	$203,290	$253,412	$304,935	$380,118
	20	$506,364	$815,895	$759,546	$1,223,842
$1,834	10	$270,955	$337,760	$406,433	$506,640
	20	$674,906	$1,087,464	$1,012,359	$1,631,197

The above is hypothetical. Interest rates and returns do not stay level for long periods of time. Some products have fees, expenses, and risks. As a result, losses are possible with some products. This secret is not intended to provide investment advice, but it is a suggestion that you should think about your retirement savings regularly. Turn the page to learn what your next steps could be.

Your neighbors are getting a 50%-like annual return without risk. You can too.

Next Steps

- Ask HR Resources at work if you have a 401(k), if there is an employer match and how it works.

- Read everything they give you.

- Consult with your tax and legal advisors.

- Ask your tax and legal advisors for their advice on you putting your contribution into the company's stock instead of diversifying.

secret **18**

Those who act are often rewarded. Those who wait are often penalized.

W e all experience anxiety before buying a financial product. Far too often, we say to the party presenting the financial product to us, "Sounds great, but let me think about it." And, that is the right thing to say if you do want to think about it.

Unfortunately, many of us do not think about it and we never buy. When you turn the page, you will see a chart of some of the biggest buying opportunities lost as a result of anxiety and not acting.

Those who act are often rewarded. Those who wait are often penalized.

W aiting for the good times can be costly... very costly. On the opposite page, we list many of the economic and political crises that kept many consumers from acting and buying a financial product. Although these events kept some on the sidelines, some consumers acted in spite of these events. Many of those who acted were rewarded as the economy, evidenced by the Dow Jones Industrial Average^SM in the far right column, continued to move up and down, but in an upward fashion.

While history is no indication of the future, we can do one of two things. We can wait or we can act. What would you like to do?

Results Some People Got By Acting

Event	Date	DJIA	1 yr. later	Jan.2, 2014*
The Depression	10/29/29	230	-17%	7,107%
Pearl Harbor	12/07/41	116	-1%	14,190%
JFK Assassination	11/22/63	711	25%	2,231%
Vietnam Conflict	02/26/65	903	5%	1,735%
73-74 Bear Market	01/12/73	1,039	-19%	1,495%
Reagan Shot	03/30/81	992	17%	1,571%
Mkt. Plummets 22.61%	10/19/87	1,738	23%	895%
Gulf War	07/03/90	2,912	1%	469%
Oklahoma Bombing	04/19/95	4,207	32%	294%
DJIA Falls 554 Points	10/27/97	7,161	17%	131%
Terrorist Attack	09/11/01	9,606	-11%	67%
Iraq War Begins	03/19/03	8,265	23%	101%
Terrorism Escalates	03/11/04	10,128	6%	64%
N. Korean Nuclear Test	08/29/05	11,858	19%	40%
Dow Jones Closing High	10/09/07	14,165	-39%	17%
Bear Stearns Collapse	03/17/08	11,972	-38%	39%
Fed Takeover of F. Mae	09/07/08	11,511	-17%	44%
GM Fails after 101 Yrs	06/01/09	8,721	16%	90%
European Crisis	08/08/11	10,810	22%	53%

The Dow opened on January 2, 2014 at 16,576.66

What is best for you depends upon your circumstances. Turn the page to learn what your next steps could be. This secret is not investment advice, but it is a suggestion that you should think about your retirement savings regularly.

Those who act are often rewarded. Those who wait are often penalized.

Next Steps

- Consult with your tax and legal advisors.

- Reach out to your insurance professionals for retirement alternatives.

- Circle back to your tax and legal advisors before you purchase any product or security.

- Take cautious baby steps.

- Diversify.

- Understand what you are about to buy.

- Read everything before signing.

secret

What you do in the first five years of retirement controls if you go broke or leave a legacy.

Professors and actuaries know it, some insurance professionals know it, but some of the nicest Grandads and Grandmoms in America do not know that what happens in the first three to five years of their retirement will control whether they are part of welfare or living in a gorgeous home near the 18th fairway. If you are a nice Grandad or Grandmom, turn the page.

19 *What you do in the first five years of retirement controls if you go broke or leave a legacy.*

Longer life expectancies have changed what consumers now want and need. As a result, income planning has emerged as the number one topic among consumers concerned about outliving their money.

As a result, you must learn about Income Planning from your tax, legal, and insurance professional. After all, it is your life and some of the decisions you make early on during retirement, surprisingly, can control where you live, with whom you live, and how you live, and unfairly, how some of our adult children and grandchildren will remember us.

Challenge: When is the best time to take a withdrawal? On the opposite page, we show one very common mistake, taking too much money out too soon. In the example on the following page, we have a male age 65 who is getting a before tax return of 4% and wishes to withdraw $5,500 beginning at the end of year one. As you can see, this individual has $15,873 remaining in year 30. In other words, no more income in a few years and no legacy for him and his spouse to leave to their children and grandchildren.

Fortunately, there is a better alternative for you and your spouse to consider. Take annual withdrawals of $5,500 after the 5th year instead. If you do just wait four extra years to year 5 before taking annual withdrawals, you will have $80,625 instead of $15,873; 400% more money because you tightened your belt and you saw a few less movies and had less dinners at sit-down restaurants after 5 p.m. during those first five years.

We also unveil on the opposite page, the impact of a loss in the first year of retirement compared to gain in the first year. As you will see, there is an unbelievable difference between a 4% gain in year 1 of retirement and a 35% loss in year 1 of retirement even when we keep annual withdrawals beginning at the same time, and returns after the first year identical. Said differently, a 35% loss, a loss too many experienced in 2008-2009, resulted in the individual going broke in year 16 if they began withdrawals in year 1.

What You Do In The Beginning Years Of Retirement Controls If You Go Broke Or Leave A Legacy

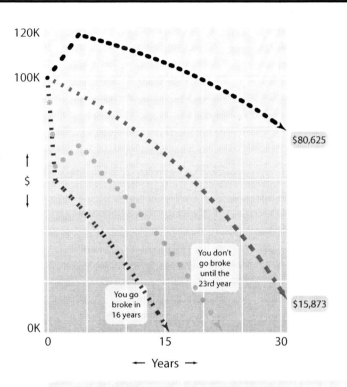

▬ ▬ ➤	$5,500 annual withdrawals after first year at 4% interest
● ● ● ➤	$5,500 annual withdrawals after fifth year at 4% interest
▪ ▪ ▪ ▪ ◨➤	$5,500 annual withdrawals after first year with a 35% first year loss and 4% interest thereafter
● ● ● ➤	$5,500 annual withdrawals after fifth year with a 35% first year loss and 4% interest thereafter

The above is hypothetical and is for illustrative purposes only. The manner in which assets deplete to zero or accumulate are approximate and are based on a hypothetical interest rate. Interest rates and returns do not stay level for long periods of time. Some products have fees, expenses, and risks. As a result, losses are possible with some products. What is best for you depends upon your circumstances. Turn the page to learn what your next steps could be. This secret and all of the other secrets in this book are not intended to provide investment advice.

What you do in the first five years of retirement controls if you go broke or leave a legacy.

Next Steps
- Consult with your tax and legal advisor.

- If you do not want to outlive your money, ask your insurance or investment professional to illustrate "what if scenarios" using Income Planning software. Ask for scenarios that can assume withdrawals later instead of now like on the previous page. And, more importantly, ask for "what if scenarios" that can assume negative returns in the early years.

- Circle back to your tax and legal advisors before purchasing any product or security.

Important Question:

Since none of us has a crystal ball, no one knows if the next 35% annual loss like in 2008-2009 is around the corner. In case you do suffer a 35% loss in your first year of retirement, do you have other assets?

If not, would you like to learn how to side step a 35% loss by getting 0% in the bad years and a percentage of the increases in an external index in the good years? If so, take Secret 71 to your tax and legal advisors and ask for their opinion since they know you and your circumstances better than we.

Unfortunately, too many move their IRA dollars the second best way instead of *the best* way.

There are now over 4 trillion dollars in Individual Retirement Accounts, in 401(k)s, and 1 trillion dollars in ROTH accounts. With more pension plans being terminated, less employer matching for 401(k)s, and all of the press given to ROTH Conversions, an unprecedented amount of concerned U.S. taxpayers need to learn the best way to move, transfer, and rollover their dollars without unnecessary income taxation and IRS penalties. To learn whether you should use the IRA Rollover or the IRA Transfer, just turn the page.

20 *Unfortunately, too many move their IRA dollars the second best way instead of the best way.*

The IRS gives you two ways to move qualified plan money and you should know how to move qualified money since the government is making it so easy for you do it the right way.

3 things we should know about an IRA Rollover:

1. It is a tax–advantaged way to reposition qualified money that has never been taxed.

2. IRA Rollovers can be preceded by the owner taking constructive receipt of the dollars and taxes will still be deferred if these dollars are "rolled over" within 60 days. A federal and state withholding tax of 20% will apply. The federal and state taxes withheld can be regained by adding an amount equivalent to the federal and state income taxes withheld to the amount received from your distribution when you rollover your funds within 60 days.

3. You can "rollover" Traditional and SEP IRAs dollars only once per 12 month period.

4 things we should know about an IRA Transfer:

1. There is no limit on how many times money can be repositioned if you use the IRA Transfer.

2. Owner never receives constructive receipt.

3. Dollars are transferred from trustee of the old plan to trustee of the new plan (trustee to trustee). It can be that simple.

4. No taxes are withheld from Transfer.

Which one is the best way? Since interest rates and the stock market can plummet or skyrocket and emergencies almost always occur unexpectedly, it makes sense to have no limit on how many times you can reposition your qualified money. If you and your tax and legal advisors agree, and they know you best, then an IRA Transfer is worthy of your consideration.

Disclaimer: All parties are strongly urged to consult their tax advisors since W.V.H., Inc. is not qualified to provide tax advice and tax changes may be "around the corner!"

The Differences Between An IRA Rollover And An IRA Transfer

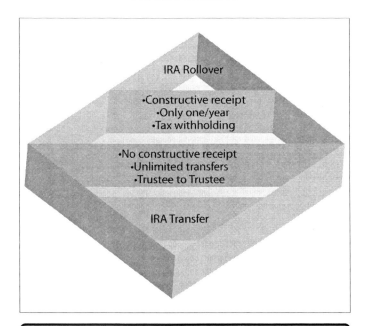

IRA Rollover

•Constructive receipt
•Only one/year
•Tax withholding

•No constructive receipt
•Unlimited transfers
•Trustee to Trustee

IRA Transfer

In all instances, always consult with your tax advisor

What is best for you depends upon your circumstances. Turn the page to learn what your next steps could be. This secret is not investment advice, but it is a suggestion that you should think about your retirement savings regularly.

Unfortunately, too many move their IRA dollars the second best way instead of the best way.

Next Steps

- Consult with your tax and legal advisor.
- Circle back to your tax and legal advisors before purchasing any product or security.

secret **21**

Excess withdrawals from a retirement account is the #1 reason why retirees go broke.

Many of us can control how we live during retirement by just learning from some of the common mistakes that consumers make at the onset of retirement. Fortunately, these common mistakes can often be easily avoided. The next page unveils the slight difference between going broke far too soon and leaving $100,000 to your loved ones.

21 *Excess withdrawals from a retirement account is the #1 reason why retirees go broke.*

H ow much income should be withdrawn especially in the early years of retirement?

One very common mistake is taking too much money out too soon. In the example on the following page, we have a couple who are getting a before tax return of 6% and they wish to withdraw $10,000 beginning at the end of year one.

As you can see, this couple runs out of money in 16 years. In other words, no more income for themselves and no legacy to leave to their children and grandchildren.

Another alternative would be to withdraw $8,000 a year instead of $10,000 a year. If that were done, the couple would run out of money in 24 years instead of 16 years.

Fortunately, there is a better alternative for you and your spouse to consider. Take annual withdrawals of $1,000 instead. In other words, tighten the belt; a few less movies and a few less dinners out after 5:00 PM.

When you do, you can potentially receive annual income of $1,000 forever instead of $10,000 for 16 years. Said differently, you can potentially receive lifetime income plus leave a legacy for your loved ones...all because you avoided taking excess withdrawals.

How Much You Withdraw Affects Your Heirs

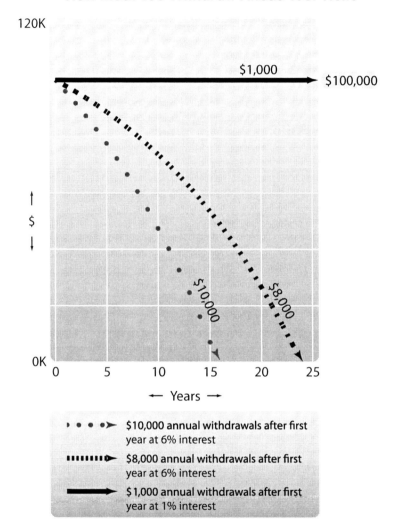

- ▸ • • •➤ $10,000 annual withdrawals after first year at 6% interest
- ▪▪▪▪▪▪▪➤ $8,000 annual withdrawals after first year at 6% interest
- ➤ $1,000 annual withdrawals after first year at 1% interest

The above is hypothetical and is for illustrative purposes only. The manner in which assets deplete to zero or accumulate are approximate and are based on a hypothetical interest rate. Interest rates and returns do not stay level for long periods of time. Some products have fees, expenses, and risks. As a result, losses are possible with some products. What is best for you depends upon your circumstances. Turn the page to learn what your next steps could be. This secret and all of the other secrets in this book are not intended to provide investment advice.

Excess withdrawals from a retirement account is the #1 reason why retirees go broke.

Next Steps

- Consult with your tax and legal advisor.

- Reach out to your insurance and/or investment professional for products that can provide you annual income.

- Circle back to your tax and legal advisors before purchasing any products or security.

- Take cautious baby steps.

- Diversify.

- Understand what you are about to buy.

- Read everything before you sign your name.

The best place to get income is from an insurer if you are in the right tax bracket.

Y ou must either learn more about Income Planning from your tax, legal, and insurance professional or by yourself via books, newspapers, seminars, web conferences, and websites. After all, it is your life and some of the decisions you make early on during retirement, surprisingly and unfairly, can control where you live, with whom you live, how you live, and unfairly, how your adult children and grandchildren could remember you.

22

The best place to get income is from an insurer if you are in the right tax bracket.

As someone famous once said, the eighth wonder of the world is compound interest. And, this comparison proves that they were right. In the example on the opposite page, we compare $100,000 in a taxable alternative to money in a tax-deferred annuity for an individual in a 35% tax bracket pre-retirement and in a 15% tax bracket during retirement. The illustration assumes that both alternatives accumulate over a 15 year period of time with withdrawals of $13,000 beginning after the 15th year. As you see, the individual will run out of money with the taxable alternative much earlier than with the tax-deferred annuity.

As you can see, the tax-deferred alternative can potentially provide annual income longer than the taxable alternative, not to mention a potentially much larger legacy for the surviving spouse, children, and grandchildren.

Surprisingly, the advantage of the tax-deferred alternative still exists, but lessens more than one might expect when a 35% tax bracket is assumed during retirement.

When you begin to ask your insurance professional for two side-by-side comparisons, comparing taxable and tax-deferred alternatives, you can appreciate the power of tax deferral.

The Differences Between A 15% And 35% Tax Bracket At Retirement

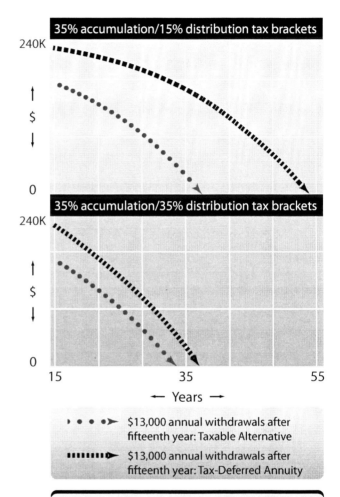

35% accumulation/15% distribution tax brackets

240K

↑ $ ↓

0

35% accumulation/35% distribution tax brackets

240K

↑ $ ↓

0

15   35   55

← Years →

• • • •► $13,000 annual withdrawals after fifteenth year: Taxable Alternative

■■■■■■■► $13,000 annual withdrawals after fifteenth year: Tax-Deferred Annuity

The interest rates for the Tax-Deferred Fixed Annuities are hypothetical since interest rates vary by product and carrier. All parties should see the insurer disclosure and annuity contract for guaranteed interest rates and values. Bank CDs are insured up to applicable limits by the FDIC. Annuities are insurance products and are NOT insured by the FDIC or any other federal government agency. The guarantees in an annuity contract are subject to the claims-paying ability of the insurer making the guarantees. Annuities have earnings which are taxable upon withdrawal and, if taken before age 59.5, may be subject to IRS penalties. Withdrawals taken during the Surrender Charge period above the penalty-free amount will be subject to Surrender Charges and a possible Market Value Adjustment. All parties should consult with their tax advisors.

The above is hypothetical and is for illustrative purposes only.

22 *The best place to get income is from an insurer if you are in the right tax bracket.*

Next Steps

- Consult with your tax and legal advisor.

- Reach out to your insurance and/or investment professional for products that can provide you annual income.

- Circle back to your tax and legal advisors before purchasing any products or security.

- Take cautious baby steps.

- Diversify.

- Understand what you are about to buy.

- Read everything before you sign your name.

A one time $2,000 gift to a baby born today could be worth $1,000,000.

W ould you like to help your next grandchild or child become a millionaire? All you need is time, a good return, and a special tax advantage. Simply turn the page to learn what that tax advantage is.

23 *A one time $2,000 gift to a baby born today could be worth $1,000,000.*

O n the opposite page, we show the impact that a very small one time gift of $2,000 can have if you have time (65 years), an unreasonable to expect return like 10%, and a tax advantage like tax deferral.

The chart also shows how much money can accumulate when you make a one time premium of $100,000 or annual payments of $12,000 at various interest rates and over different periods of time.

How Money Can Grow Tax-Deferred

Single Payments			
Amount	**%**	**Years**	**Value**
One time gift of $2,000	10%	65	$980,741
Single premium of $100,000	1%	20	$122,019
Single premium of $100,000	3%	20	$180,611
Single premium of $100,000	5%	20	$265,330
Annual Payments			
Annual premium of $12,000	5%	5	$69,623
Annual premium of $12,000	5%	15	$271,890
Annual premium of $12,000	5%	25	$601,632
Monthy Payments			
Monthy premium of $1,000	3%	5	$64,481
Monthy premium of $1,000	3%	15	$227,540
Monthy premium of $1,000	3%	25	$447,123

The above is hypothetical. Interest rates and returns do not stay level for long periods of time. Some products have fees, expenses, and risks. As a result, losses are possible with some products. This secret is not intended to provide investment advice, but it is a suggestion that you should think about your retirement savings regularly. Turn the page to learn what your next steps could be.

A one time $2,000 gift to a baby born today could be worth $1,000,000.

Solutions to Consider:

- Ascertain your tolerance for risk. If you would come home "looking for the dog to kick" if you lost 10%-30% of your money in one year, stay away from seeking annual returns of 10%-12%.

- Determine your time horizon. When are you most apt to need some or all of your money?

- Be prepared for emergencies. Make sure you have, at least, 6 months' income tucked away in highly liquid FDIC insured accounts like 30-90 day CDs, Money Market accounts or passbook savings.

Next Steps

- Consult with your tax and legal advisors on how tax deferral will affect you.

- Call your insurance professional since they have software that can create "what if" scenarios where you can see the impact that varying interest rates, different time horizons, and one time or annual payments can have on your hopes and dreams.

Inflation during retirement is the #1 risk.

While this book looks at inflation 5* different ways, this secret uncovers the crippling impact that inflation can have when you attempt to increase your retirement income each year by 3%. Fortunately, you can do something about it by turning the page now.

Secrets 15, 24, 26, and 45 look at inflation in a different way.

24 *Inflation during retirement is the #1 risk.*

Inflation has had a devastating affect on the retirement dreams of too many. In this example, we have a male age 65 receiving 4% interest, and he wants to begin taking annual withdrawals of $4,000.

As you can see, he will be able to receive $4,000 for each year of his life. On the other hand, if he were to increase his annual withdrawals by the rate of inflation such as 3% and 5%, he would go broke in years 16 and 18 respectively.

Do you want to leave a legacy to your children and grandchildren? Do you want to keep pace with inflation? If so, begin saving more money by using taxable and tax-deferred alternatives.

One "sad" alternative is to withdraw a level $4,000 and keep the $100,000 intact for you, your spouse, and children. Why is this "sad"? Your $4,000 will not keep up with inflation. One "smart" alternative is to try to accumulate more money before retirement so there will be enough assets to last longer.

The Impact Of Withdrawing More Money Each Year To Keep Up With Inflation

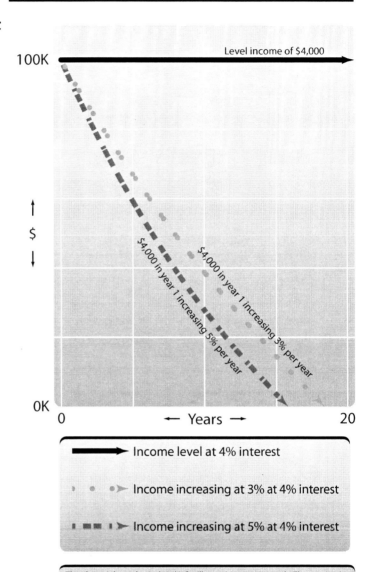

Level income of $4,000

100K

↑ $ ↓

$4,000 in year 1 increasing 5% per year

$4,000 in year 1 increasing 3% per year

0K

0 ← Years → 20

Income level at 4% interest

Income increasing at 3% at 4% interest

Income increasing at 5% at 4% interest

The above is hypothetical and is for illustrative purposes only. The manner in which assets deplete to zero or accumulate are approximate and are based on a hypothetical interest rate. Interest rates and returns do not stay level for long periods of time. Some products have fees, expenses, and risks. As a result, losses are possible with some products. What is best for you depends upon your circumstances. Turn the page to learn what your next steps could be. This secret and all of the other secrets in this book are not intended to provide investment advice.

Inflation during retirement is the #1 risk.

Next Steps

- Consult with your tax and legal advisors.

- Reach out to your insurance and/or investment professional for products that can provide you annual income.

- Circle back to your tax and legal advisors before purchasing any products or security.

- Take cautious baby steps.

- Diversify.

- Understand what you are about to buy.

- Read everything before you sign your name.

secret

The IRS allows people 50 and older to catch up and contribute an extra $5,500 to their 401(k).

Almost 50% of all employers in the private sector offer a defined contribution pension plan including 401(k)-type plans to their employees[1]. As a result, many employees can defer current income taxes on $17,500 in wages for 2014. However, if you are age 50 or older, you can defer a lot more. If you would like to see the difference between saving $23,000 a year and $17,500 a year, turn the page.

[1] *Source U.S. Department of Labor's National Compensation Survey: Employee Benefits in the United States, March 2009, 47 percent of private-sector establishments offer a defined contribution plan, which includes 401(k)-type plans.*
[2] *In 2012, the additional contribution will be indexed for inflation*

25

The IRS allows people 50 and older to catch up and contribute an extra $5,500 to their 401(k).

W ith 401(k) plans, the employee simply asks the employer to contribute some of their wages into one or more of the investment accounts that are part of the 401(k) plan. These deferred wages are not subject to federal tax withholding, accumulate tax-deferred, and are not reflected as taxable income until withdrawn. The wages that you defer (elective deferrals) are 100% vested and the investment gains are not subject to federal income taxes until distributed from the plan.

With some 401(k) plans, there are other advantages such as additional employer contributions.

Most employers make an additional contribution as well[1]; one example would be matching where an employer will match, for example, 50 cents[2] for every dollar you save, for example, up to 6 percent of pay; employer contributions, understandably, come with a vesting schedule.

There are many advantages to becoming older and one of them is being allowed to "catch up" and save more:

401(k) participants age 50 or older can make larger contributions than the "kids" age 49 and younger. On the opposite page, we compare saving pre-tax elective deferrals of $17,500 a year—the 2014 maximum for those age 49 and younger to $23,000 a year—the 2014 maximum for those age 50 and older over a 20 year period with hypothetical annual returns of 4% and at 8%. As you can see, you can have $271,570 more dollars if you agree to set aside $23,000 a year instead of $17,500. Said differently, by just setting aside an extra $5,500 a year for 20 years, you can have 271,570 more dollars.

---

1 *The Profit Sharing/401(k) Council of America's 52nd Annual Survey of Profit Sharing and 401(k) Plans: Reflecting 2008 Plan Experience reports that 5.9 percent of the companies surveyed provide no company contribution (matching or other), so approximately 95 percent of the companies included in the survey do provide some sort of contribution. This survey included 908 plans with 7.4 million participants and $600 billion in plan assets.*

2 *Employee Benefit Research Institute: Typically, the average matching rate is $.50 on the dollar up to 6 percent of pay.*

The Accumulation Power Of Saving More Using What The IRS Calls A Catch-Up Contribution

	$17,500*		$23,000**	
Yr	4%	8%	4%	8%
1	$17,824	$18,156	$23,426	$23,862
5	$96,686	$107,154	$127,073	$140,830
10	$214,739	$266,796	$282,228	$350,645
20	$534,877	$858,987	$702,983	$1,128,953

* $1,458.33 a month maximum for employees younger than age 50

** $1,916.66 a month maximum catch-up contributions of $5,500 annually for workers over age 50

The 4% and 8% returns are hypothetical; Depending upon where you save or invest your 401(k) contribution, losses are possible.

The above is hypothetical. Interest rates and returns do not stay level for long periods of time. Some products have fees, expenses, and risks. As a result, losses are possible with some products. What is best for you depends upon your circumstances. Turn the page to learn what your next steps could be. This secret is not investment advice, but it is a suggestion that you should think about your retirement savings regularly.

The IRS allows people 50 and older to catch up and contribute an extra $5,500 to their 401(k).

Next Steps

- Ask HR Resources at work if they have a 401(k), if there is an employer match, how it works, and when you can "catch up" by making additional contributions.

- Read everything they give you.

- Consult with your tax and legal advisors.

- Ask your tax and legal advisors for their advice regarding you putting your contribution into the company's stock instead of carefully diversifying.

Inflation has averaged 4.3% since 1973.

Inflation can be more devastating than a major tax increase or even a 20% loss of principal. Unfortunately, too many consumers do not take inflation into account when they plan for retirement. Should you assume inflation? Yes! Should you assume a 1% to 3% annual inflation rate? No! What should you assume? You should assume 4.3% and the reason is on the next page.

26 *Inflation has averaged 4.3% since 1973.*

S ince we license our ideas to large insurance companies and mutual fund companies, we are often asked to send them hard copy of our ideas so that their legal staff can approve, edit, or reject*. It is common for their compliance officer to recommend that we never assume an inflation rate higher than 3%. While their intentions are good since the assumption of a higher rate of inflation would encourage you to make a larger premium or investment, the assumption of a lower rate of inflation might be devastating. Please see Secrets 15, 24, 32, 35, and especially Secret 45.

So what rate of inflation should you assume? The answer is 4.3%. Why 4.3%? As you can see on the opposite page, inflation has averaged 4.3% from 1973 to 2013.

Since inflation in 2013 was only 1.2%, is inflation now under control? As President Reagan once said, "Inflation is like a virus in the bloodstream. Sometimes active, sometimes dormant, but leaving the patient weaker after every new attack."

*While it will be impossible for all or even most legal departments of insurance companies to agree on all 75 Secrets in this book, we are hoping that a few secrets will survive unchanged. This becomes another reason why you should always consult with your tax and legal advisors first since we are not planning to ask our corporate clients to approve.

Inflation 1973 To 2013

1973	8.7	1983	3.8	1993	2.7	2003	1.9
1974	12.3	1984	3.9	1994	2.7	2005	3.3
1975	6.9	1985	3.8	1995	2.5	2006	3.4
1976	4.9	1986	1.1	1996	3.3	2006	2.5
1977	6.7	1987	4.4	1997	1.7	2007	4.1
1978	9	1988	4.4	1998	1.6	2008	0.1
1979	13.3	1989	4.6	1999	2.7	2009	2.7
1980	12.5	1990	6.1	2000	3.4	2010	1.5
1981	8.9	1991	3.1	2001	1.6	2011	3
1982	3.8	1992	2.9	2002	2.4	2012	2
2013	1.5	2014	X	2015	X	2016	X

Average inflation is the total of all annual percentages added together divided by the number of years in the period specified.
In this example, the answer is 174.5 ÷ 41 = 4.29%.
The above numbers represent the CPI-U.
Source: ftp://ftp.bls.gov/pub/special.request/cpicpiai.txt

What is best for you depends upon your circumstances. Turn the page to learn what your next steps could be. This secret is not investment advice, but it is a suggestion that you should think about your retirement savings regularly.

Inflation has averaged 4.3% since 1973.

Next Steps

- Consult with your tax and legal advisors.
- Reach out to your insurance professional regarding products that can lessen the impact of inflation.
- Circle back to your tax and legal advisors regarding the products that you are considering.
- Take cautious baby steps.
- Diversify.
- Understand the product that you are about to buy.
- Read what you are about to sign.

Banks, insurers, and mutual funds can help you pay yourself first.

There are some secrets in this book that can single-handedly change your life. This secret is one of those secrets since it addresses how important it is to save regularly. However, we are not the only ones who want you to pay yourself first, others do as well. Banks, mutual funds, and insurance companies all have special programs where your money can be easily repositioned from your checking or savings account to the CD, Mutual Fund, or Flexible Premium annuity you want. Just turn the page to see how much richer your life can be once you begin paying yourself first.

27 *Banks, insurers, and mutual funds can help you pay yourself first.*

On the opposite page, we show the wisdom of paying yourself first every week, every month, or every year. Look at the difference between weekly contributions versus an annual payment.

Not too long ago, we produced a short 2 minute film titled *Paying Yourself First* about my definition of wealth when I was a kid in Atlantic City. The film also contains a few clips from when I was a young Dad with my daughter Elizabeth.

To see this film, go to www.75secrets.com. The script for the film is below. Please read it now since the words can help you so much.

"When I was growing up as a kid, some of my friends' Dads and Moms were rich, real rich. While they all kind of looked like my family—well, almost all of them—these families were different, very different. They had discretionary money. Their income exceeded their expenses. In other words, they had more money coming in than going out. As a result, their kids played and played instead of worked and worked. They had money—a lot of money.

One of my friends once told me how his family did it. They paid themselves first every payday before paying other bills. They made money first, then spent what was left over. They made buying decisions with their head, not with their heart. And they taught their children the advantages of planning for retirement by paying themselves first every payday.

As a result, these families eventually had enough assets to enjoy retirement. So, if you want paradise to be part of your future, consider planning for your future and for the future of your family by paying yourself first. Sounds like a good idea, doesn't it?"

How Much Can You Save By Paying Yourself First?

Amount/ period	4%	8%	10%
$100/year*			
10 yrs	$1,396	$1,779	$2,011
20 yrs	$3,315	$5,407	$6,972
30 yrs	$6,156	$13,240	$19,838
40 yrs	$10,362	$30,150	$53,210
$100/month**			
10 yrs	$14,873	$18,515	$20,754
20 yrs	$36,900	$59,393	$76,670
30 yrs	$69,733	$150,128	$228,031
40 yrs	$118,691	$351,527	$637,779
$100/week***			
10 yrs	$64,111	$79,941	$89,700
20 yrs	$159,601	$257,612	$333,227
30 yrs	$302,051	$652,991	$995,111
40 yrs	$514,558	$1,532,847	$2,794,050

* Compounded Annually
** Compounded Monthly
*** Compounded Daily

The above is hypothetical. Interest rates and returns do not stay level for long periods of time. Some products have fees, expenses, and risks. As a result, losses are possible with some products. This secret is not intended to provide investment advice, but it is a suggestion that you should think about your retirement savings regularly. Turn the page to learn what your next steps could be.

Banks, insurers, and mutual funds can help you pay yourself first.

Next Steps

- Consult with your tax and legal advisors.

- Reach out to your insurance professional regarding products that can help you save or invest.

- Circle back to your tax and legal advisors regarding the products that you are considering.

- Take cautious baby steps.

- Diversify.

- Understand the product that you are about to buy.

- Read what you are about to sign.

secret **28**

Turn your financial pyramid upside down when nearing retirement.

T he financial pyramid has long been accepted as an effective way to communicate the importance of diversifying your money among different asset classes. Sadly, the financial pyramid always has the same look and feel with the majority of the "safe and secure" assets being at the base of the pyramid. However, should a son or daughter's financial pyramid look like their Mom and Dad's? Turn the page to see what your financial pyramid could look like.

Turn your financial pyramid upside down when nearing retirement.

A s you will see at the top of the opposite page, the financial pyramid for consumers 55 years and older suggests that the majority of retirement assets should be "very secure" or "secure" assets shown as the foundation of the pyramid. The theory correctly assumes that the closer you are to retirement, the less time you have to recover from losses or surprises.

However, just as people age 55 and older have less time to recover, "young whippersnappers" age 21-54 have more time to recover from losses, surprises, and things going the wrong way. As a result, one could say that their financial pyramid should be turned upside down and they should have less dollars in assets known to accumulate at single digit interest rates.

The Amount Of Money You Should Have In Secure And Very Safe Alternatives

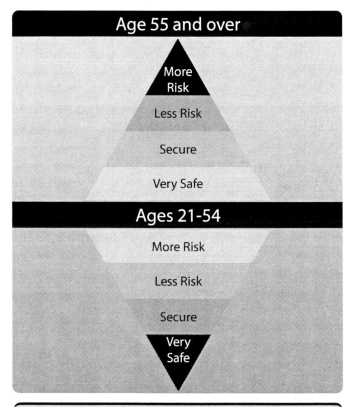

What is best for you depends upon your circumstances. Turn the page to learn what your next steps could be. This secret is not investment advice, but it is a suggestion that you should think about your retirement savings regularly.

Turn your financial pyramid upside down when nearing retirement.

Next Steps

- Consult with your tax and legal advisors and ask them to recommend the type of assets that should go into each section of your financial pyramid.

- Reach out to your insurance/investment professionals. Discuss with your insurance professionals the type of products that they feel are best for you. They call it product suitability, which can be easily done by you answering a series of questions.

- With your investment professional, have an open dialogue about asset allocation and other ways for you to diversify your money.

- Remember: When you do diversify, you are less apt to be seriously affected if interest rates, returns, promises, and expectations go in the wrong direction.

A cup of coffee really costs you $43,580 if you remain a spender.

A cup of Joe every morning is *not* a better alternative to running out of money during retirement. If you were to save that $3.49 that you give to your barista every morning, you could have $43,580 tucked away in 20 years in a nice account. Turn the page to see what other products and services really cost you.

A cup of coffee really costs you $43,580 if you remain a spender.

There are spenders and there are savers. On the opposite page, we show how much extra money you would have during retirement if you saved instead of spent. Said differently, if you redirected the $1,256 that you give to your favorite coffee shop every year to a retirement account yielding 5% interest every year for 20 years, you would have $43,580 before taxes.

But, there are other rewards, dates, getaways, and holiday presents that can be converted to assets. Some are listed below and on the opposite page. Are we suggesting that you stop enjoying life or have empty holidays? No! However, we do ask you to set your priorities on what is more important to you. Having front row tickets to see the Yankees play now or two seats to Miley's final performance later?

Which of these luxuries are more important to you than,
a) protecting the people that you love by owning more life and heath insurance, or b) having more money later:

- Having lunch outside of work instead of paper-bagging your lunch?

- Having access to 287 TV stations instead of 99?

- Seeing an NFL game live instead of on TV?

secret (29)

What Happens If You Convert What You Spend Into Saving?

Product/Reward	Cost	Annual Cost	Value in 20 years*
Daily cup of coffee	$3.49	$1,256	$43,580
Movie for two every weekend (including soda and popcorn)	$38	$1,976	$68,605
Jewelry every anniversary	$3,000	$3,000	$104,158
Weekend getaway every 3 months	$1,000	$4,000	$138,877

*Assumes a before tax return of 5% interest over a 20 year period

The above is hypothetical. Interest rates and returns do not stay level for long periods of time. Some products have fees, expenses, and risks. As a result, losses are possible with some products. This secret is not intended to provide investment advice, but it is a suggestion that you should think about your retirement savings regularly. Turn the page to learn what your next steps could be.

29 *A cup of coffee really costs you $43,580 if you remain a spender.*

Next Steps

- Consult with your tax and legal advisors.

- Reach out to your insurance professional regarding products that can help you save and/or invest.

- Circle back to your tax and legal advisors regarding the products that you are considering.

- Take cautious baby steps.

- Diversify.

- Understand the product that you are about to buy.

- Read what you are about to sign.

Review the Social Security Statement with your professionals.

In the past, 90 days before your birthday, the Social Security Administration would mail you a FREE personalized statement about you and your retirement. Few consumers read this report. Those who read it did not understand it. Due to budget restrictions, your statement will no longer be mailed to you. However, you can get your statement online by simply creating an account online at www.socialsecurity.gov. The solution? Ask your insurance professional to review it with you.

Review the Social Security Statement with your professionals.

I f you read your Social Security Statement, you will learn all of the following :

From **Page 2**, you will learn if you have qualified for benefits:

If so, how much your monthly payment would be if you stopped working at

age 62	$_____
at full retirement age	$_____
at age 70	$_____

whether you have qualified for disability benefits and, if so, how much..$_____

You will also learn if you are qualified so your family receives survivor benefits. If so, you'll learn

if you die this year, what certain members of your family would receive:

Your child	$_____
Your spouse who is caring for your child	$_____
Your spouse who reaches full retirement age	$_____
Total family benefits	$_____
Special one time death benefit	$_____

Middle Insert of Your Social Security Statement

You will learn important things to consider before you retire and how to get more information

From **Page 3,** you will see total Social Security and Medicare taxes paid over your working career.

Estimated taxes paid for Social Security
You paid:..$_____
Your employers paid:..$_____

Estimated taxes paid for Medicare
You paid:..$_____
Your employers paid:..$_____

(Continued on page 122)

Your Social Security Statement

Prevent identity theft—protect your Social Security number

Prepared especially for William V. Harris

June 2, 2009

www.socialsecurity.gov

See inside for your personal information →

William V. Harris

What's inside...

What Social Security Means To You

This *Social Security Statement* can help you plan for your financial future. It provides estimates of your Social Security benefits under current law and updates your latest reported earnings.

Please read this *Statement* carefully. If you see a mistake, please let us know. That's important because your benefits will be based on our record of your lifetime earnings. We recommend you keep a copy of your *Statement* with your financial records.

Social Security is for people of all ages...
We're more than a retirement program. Social Security also can provide benefits if you become disabled and help support your family after you die.

Work to build a secure future...
Social Security is the largest source of income for most elderly Americans today, but Social Security was never intended to be your only source of income when you retire. You also will need other savings, investments, pensions or retirement accounts to make sure you have enough money to live comfortably when you retire.

Saving and investing wisely are important not only for you and your family, but for the entire country. If you want to learn more about how and why to save, you should visit www.*mymoney.gov*, a federal government website dedicated to teaching all Americans the basics of financial management.

About Social Security's future...
Social Security is a compact between generations. For decades, America has kept the promise of security for its workers and their families. Now, however, the Social Security system is facing serious financial problems, and action is needed soon to make sure the system will be sound when today's younger workers are ready for retirement.

In 2017 we will begin paying more in benefits than we collect in taxes. Without changes, by 2041 the Social Security Trust Fund will be exhausted* and there will be enough money to pay only about 78 cents for each dollar of scheduled benefits. We need to resolve these issues soon to make sure Social Security continues to provide a foundation of protection for future generations.

Social Security on the Net...
Visit www.*socialsecurity.gov* on the Internet to learn more about Social Security. You can read our publications, use the *Social Security Benefit Calculators* to calculate future benefits or use our easy online forms to apply for benefits.

Michael J. Astrue
Commissioner

* These estimates are based on the intermediate assumptions from the Social Security Trustees' Annual Report to the Congress.

What is best for you depends upon your circumstances. Turn the page to learn what your next steps could be. This secret is not investment advice, but it is a suggestion that you should think about your retirement savings regularly.

30 *Review the Social Security Statement with your professionals.*

(Continued from page 120)

From **Page 4,** you learn important facts about Social Security

From **Page 1,** you are told 3 major things

1. You are told about a freely accessible website dedicated to teach all Americans the basics of financial management, www.mymoney.gov.

2. You are told that beginning in 2017, they will be paying more in benefits than they collect in taxes.

3. Without changes, the Social Security Trust Fund will be exhausted in 2041 with only enough money to pay 78 cents for each dollar of scheduled benefits.

Next Steps

- Understand your Social Security Statement.

- Consult with your tax and legal advisors.

- Reach out to your insurance and/or investment professional for software illustrations that allow your Social Security benefits to be entered with your present savings and investments along with your objectives so shortages or excesses are clearly visible to you.

31

Surround yourself with five mentors and be like Warren, JFK, and King Arthur.

P residents have called them "My Cabinet." Executives at major Fortune 500 companies call them "Our Board of Directors." King Arthur called them "My Round Table." Who do you have surrounding you who gives you great advice? If the answer is no one or just one person, turn the page to learn how to create a team of professionals who can collectively help you stay out of debt, accumulate more money, pay less income taxes, and lessen what inflation can do to your purchasing power.

31 Surround yourself with five mentors and be like Warren, JFK, and King Arthur.

So many consumers spend almost all of their time working and little or none of their time getting their money to work for them. However, when surveyed, almost all consumers say that their retirement will be a challenge, they pay too much for insurance, and tax breaks and tax advantages are available only to the rich.

However, if you begin to surround yourself with a team of bright unselfish professionals, your retirement can be fun, you will not have too much or too little insurance, and you can pay the least amount of income taxes allowed by tax law.

Who do you need? At the least, you need 1) an accountant, 2) an attorney, 3) insurance professionals, and 4) an investment professional.

How do you find them? The 2 best ways are to ask your friends and relatives for those who have really helped them in the tax, legal, insurance, and investment arena. If you already have some of your team built, ask them who they use for their tax, legal, insurance, or investment needs.

Are there any other ways to build a team ? While we do not recommend asking everyone who calls you to come over to your house, we do suggest that you consider meeting some of them at a nearby coffee shop or at their office for 15 minutes on a Saturday. When you combine the alternative—not meeting anyone—with the probable end result—less money—with your responsibility—taking care of your loved ones, missing some of the college football games one fall Saturday is a small price to pay.

What are you looking for? Someone who 1) listens more than talks, 2) cares about you more than themselves, 3) answers "I don't know but I can find out." if you ask them a difficult question and 4) is willing to get together with the other members of your team semi-annually where the entire and only topic is YOU.

Professionals You Want On Your Team

- Accountant

- Attorney

- Insurance Professional
  (Home, Car)

- Insurance Professional
  (Life, Health, Annuities)

- Investment Professional
  (Securities)

What is best for you depends upon your circumstances. Turn the page to learn what your next steps could be. This secret is not investment advice, but it is a suggestion that you should think about your retirement savings regularly.

31 *Surround yourself with five mentors and be like Warren, JFK, and King Arthur.*

Next Steps

- Consult with your tax and legal advisors.

- Reach out to your insurance professional regarding products that can help you think about your money.

- Circle back to your tax and legal advisors regarding the products that you are considering.

- Take cautious baby steps.

- Diversify.

- Understand the product that you are about to buy.

- Read what you are about to sign.

A night out to the movies will soon cost $340 for a family.

Almost everyone should be looking for effective ways to lessen the impact that inflation can have on their retirement dollar. On the next page, we include the script for a 2 minute online movie we produced titled *Going To The Movies* and a chart on what things could soon cost.

32

A night out to the movies will soon cost $340 for a family.

The script below is from the very popular 2 minute online film we produced titled *Going To The Movies*. Since we produced a film for every decade from the 1930s to the 1980s, the archival footage in each version is potentially award winning. Hopefully, you will feel that the words are award-winning too.

"Remember going to the movies? Mom suggesting what you should wear. Dad maybe complaining that going to the movies was becoming increasingly too expensive. And, your Dad was right. It was too expensive since $1.00 for 1 movie ticket was a lot of money back then. Plus, Dad had to get a movie ticket for everyone in the family.

But, that was only half of the story. Dad had to dip into his pocket a few more times before and during the movie. There was gas for the car, parking, candy, soda, and popcorn for the entire family. It became so increasingly expensive that a visit to the bank for a cash withdrawal preceded every movie.

Unfortunately, going to the movies continues to be increasingly expensive. In fact, if it continues its current pace, going to the movies could soon be a $340 night out on the town. $340? A $9.00 movie ticket today could double to $18 in 18 years and then to $36 in 18 years later. A $5 bag of popcorn could also double to $10 in 18 years and then to $20 18 years later. A $3 soda could increase to $6.00, then to $12. And $68 times 5, you, your spouse, your 100 year old dad, and your two 60 plus year old children equals $340.

(Continued on page 130)

What Will It Cost For A Family of 5 To Go To The Movies?

	Today	In 18 years	In 36 years
Ticket	$11	$22	$44
Popcorn	$5	$10	$20
Soda	$3	$6	$12
Per person	$19	$38	$76
	x5	x5	x5
Total	$95	$190	$380

Assumes a 4% inflation rate

The above is hypothetical. This secret is not intended to provide investment advice, but it is a suggestion that you should think about your retirement savings regularly. Turn the page to learn what your next steps could be.

32 *A night out to the movies will soon cost $340 for a family.*

(Continued from page 128)

Without a doubt, inflation and longer life expectancies can dramatically change how you live, where you live, and with whom you live. Simply put, if your money is not growing at the same rate as prices and services, you could be faced with an abrupt change. You either run out of money or you purchase less.

Do you think that prices and services will continue to increase? Would you like to learn how to keep pace with potentially increasing costs?"

Next Steps

- Consult with your tax and legal advisors.
- Reach out to your insurance professionals for ways to lessen the impact of inflation.
- Understand what you buy.
- Read what you sign.
- Diversify.

secret **33**

Almost anyone can get $50,000 a year, but for how long is the secret.

ncome Planning and Retirement Planning now go hand in hand. As a result, most insurance professionals now own sophisticated software that can create a wide variety of income planning scenarios for their clients. You name what you want in annual income, they can tell you in seconds the amount of money needed, the return needed, and more importantly, how long annual income will last. Now please turn the page to learn more.

33

Almost anyone can get $50,000 a year, but for how long is the secret.

Many Presidents of the United States have said Social Security was never designed to be your sole source of retirement income. The Social Security Administration reminds you every year in your statement that it is your job to prepare for your future. Without a doubt, longer life expectancy, above average price increases on products and services that retirees are more apt to need, and the 30%-50% losses that too many experienced in 2008 have made retirement planning more challenging. As a result, Income Planning and Retirement Planning now go hand-in-hand.

On the opposite page, we show you how easily you can get $50,000 in annual retirement income. That is easy! The hard part is getting the $50,000 to continue.

If you have only $48,000 of retirement assets, those assets will generate $50,000 for around 13 months. If you have $250,000, those assets will remain for 6 years and $500,000 will last for 15 years. And, for those of you who want to leave a nice legacy to your children and grandchildren, $1,000,000 would give you and/or your spouse annual income of $50,000 forever and $1,000,000 to your heirs assuming, of course, 5% interest.

However, there are steps that you can take now that can potentially get your assets to last longer. Just turn the page to discover your Next Steps.

How Long Will $50,000 Last?

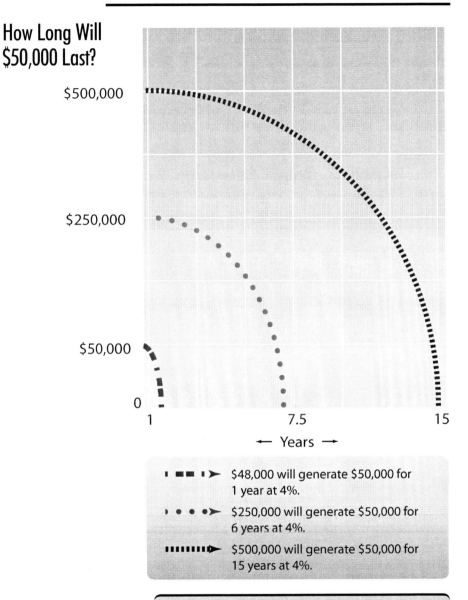

$500,000

$250,000

$50,000

0

1   7.5   15

← Years →

▪ ■■ ▪ ►	$48,000 will generate $50,000 for 1 year at 4%.
▪ ● ● ●►	$250,000 will generate $50,000 for 6 years at 4%.
▪▪▪▪▪▪▪►	$500,000 will generate $50,000 for 15 years at 4%.

The above is hypothetical and is for illustrative purposes only. The manner in which assets deplete to zero or accumulate are approximate and are based on a hypothetical interest rate. Interest rates and returns do not stay level for long periods of time. Some products have fees, expenses, and risks. As a result, losses are possible with some products. What is best for you depends upon your circumstances. Turn the page to learn what your next steps could be. This secret and all of the other secrets in this book are not intended to provide investment advice.

33 *Almost anyone can get $50,000 a year, but for how long is the secret.*

Next Steps • Consult with your tax and legal advisors and the mentors discussed in Secret 31 about:

Is 4% interest too high of an interest rate to assume?

Do you have the time to get some of your money accumulating on a tax-deferred basis? If so, do you have a tolerance for risk?

Should you consider the income that insurance companies can guarantee via Immediate Annuities or a Lifetime Income Rider?

Should you consider a new lifestyle for you with budget cuts such as less sit down restaurants, more movies in the morning, and vacations closer to home?

34

Think about your money on a quarterly basis.

Unfortunately, people do not think about their money on a regular basis. If they did, would they really have $2,000 of credit card debt paying interest rates of 18%-22% when they have $2,000 tucked away at the bank earning 1%? If they thought about their money regularly, they would get that $2,000 at the bank and pay off that $2,000 of credit card debt and immediately be 17%-21% richer. Turn the page if you are ready to begin thinking about your money on a regular basis.

34 *Think about your money on a quarterly basis.*

Obe of the greatest things that insurance professionals do when they get together with you is to help you think about your money on a regular basis. When we were all growing up, our parents told us never to put all of our eggs in one basket. But, in spite of that, too many of us still put too much of our money in one given product or concept. Therefore, one of the major responsibilities of an insurance professional is to help you think about your money before you retire and during your retirement.

The bottom line is that you owe it to your spouse, to your children and, maybe, to your grandchildren to be the best that you can be. And, thinking about your money regularly is your job.

In addition, as you can see on the opposite page, you need tax and legal advisors and insurance professionals who care about you, listen more than talk, tell a story of diversification, want you to take cautious baby steps, want you to know the advantages and disadvantages, and will help you understand your tolerance for risk and your time horizon.

Think About Money On a Regular Basis With Advisors and Professionals Who:

- Care about you.

- Listen more than talk.

- Tell a story of diversification.

- Want you to take baby steps.

- Want you to know the advantages and disadvantages.

- Will ascertain your tolerance for risk and your time horizon.

What is best for you depends upon your circumstances. Turn the page to learn what your next steps could be. This secret is not investment advice, but it is a suggestion that you should think about your retirement savings regularly.

34 *Think about your money on a quarterly basis.*

Next Steps

- Consult with your tax and legal advisors.

- Reach out to your insurance professional regarding products that can help you think about your money on a more regular basis.

- If you do not have an insurance professional:

    Ask your friends and neighbors if they are very, very pleased with their insurance professional.

    Reflect on who took or who is taking good care of Mom and Dad's insurance and investments.

    Agree to meet a professional who calls you at a coffee shop nearby for less than 30 minutes.

- Circle back to your tax and legal advisors regarding the products that you are considering buying.

- Take cautious baby steps.

- Diversify.

- Understand the product that you are about to buy.

- Read what you are about to sign.

secret **35**

In 1963, when Hollywood's leading ladies' man was born, a new car cost $2,494.

n 1963, a newspaper cost 7 cents, a first class stamp was 5 cents, and Volkswagen's Karmann Ghia cost $2,494. If you think that prices will be higher in 10 years than they are today, you must take the 4 steps on the next page to potentially lessen the impact that inflation can have on your retirement dollar. Send your guess to which Hollywood star was born in 1963 to wvharris@adnc.com.

RETIREMENT | 139

35 *In 1963, when Hollywood's leading ladies' man was born, a new car cost $2,494.*

O n the opposite page, we show what things cost around the time you were born. We have 3 important questions to ask you.

1. Do you think that a car, home, and newspaper will cost more 10 years from now than they do today?
2. What are you doing about this problem of yours?
3. Would you like to learn how to lessen the impact that inflation will have on your retirement dollar?

Step 1: Devote more time to thinking about your money than next summer's vacation. Not going broke during retirement or not leaving a legacy to your loved ones is a lot more important than selecting Disneyland or the Jersey shore.

Step 2: Begin selecting mentors who have your best interests in mind. See Secret 31.

Step 3: Understand what you are buying by reading the company's literature, especially the fine print, and always read what you are signing.

| What did things cost the year you were born? | | | | % of people who had... | |
Year	News-paper	1st Class Stamp	Car	Home	TV	Phone
1935	3¢	3¢	$590	$3,450	0	31.8
1940	3¢	3¢	$828	$2,938	0	36.9
1945	3¢	3¢	$1,030	$4,645	0	46.2
1950	5¢	3¢	$1,299	$7,354	9	61.8
1955	5¢	3¢	$2,395	$9,337	64.5	71.5
1960	6¢	4¢	$1,627	$11,900	87.1	78.3
1965	10¢	5¢	$1,959	$14,270	92.6	84.5
1970	10¢	6¢	$2,652	$17,000	95.3	90.5
1975	15¢	10¢	$2,999	$28,388	97.1	95
1980	25¢	15¢	$8,085	$47,200	97.9	93
1985	25¢	22¢	$8,999	$60,815	98.1	91.8

Please see what things cost the year you were born on pages 348 and 349.

Sources: W.V.H., Inc.; Annapolis Capital; Morris County Library; Department of Labor; Bureau of Labor Statistics; Board of Governors of the Federal Reserve System; U.S. Census Bureau

In 1963, when Hollywood's leading ladies' man was born, a new car cost $2,494.

Next Steps

- Write down your top 3 financial goals.

- Do something about it by reaching out to your tax and legal advisors and insurance professionals.

- Discuss money with your spouse; one of you will survive the other.

- Do not insulate your spouse or your adult children from your advisors and insurance professionals; create continuity.

Tax free may not be as good as you think.

Interest can be taxed 3 different ways: taxable, tax deferred and tax free. At first glance, tax free would appear to be the most interesting. However, it might not be as good as you think. Turn the page to learn more about taxable, tax deferred and tax free and what many municipal bondholders forget to remember during an increasing interest rate environment.

36

Tax free may not be as good as you think.

There are 3 tax flavors when saving and investing money. Each one is delicious for different reasons, however, each tax flavor comes with its own side effects.

Taxable accounts such as bank accounts are delicious since they can be FDIC insured. However, the side-effects would be the income taxes that you have to pay on the interest regardless of whether you leave it in or take it out.

Tax-deferred accounts such as Fixed and Variable Annuities are delicious since you only pay income taxes when you want to, when you withdraw the interest. However, the side-effects such as no FDIC insurance and premature withdrawal penalties, in other words, surrender charges are the price you pay for tax deferral, guarantees and your option to elect lifetime income.

Tax-free accounts such as loans and the death benefit from a life insurance policy are delicious since it helps us when we need emergency money and helps our loved ones after we die. Municipal Bonds are delicious since they provide tax-free income to taxpayers who need income. However the side-effects have been shocking for some taxpayers who saw interest rates and the claims-paying ability of the bond issuer go the wrong direction.

In 1984, interest rates were much higher than the interest rates that many bondholders were getting on the bonds that they had bought many years before. When that occurs, the selling price of the bond decreases. On the opposite page, we include a visual from one of our books. In that book, we were discussing tax-exempt Municipal Bonds and how the price of a Municipal Bond went up and down based on 2 variables: interest rates and the claims-paying ability of the issuer such the city, state, etc. As you see on the opposite page, the lower the coupon rate—meaning the initial interest rate of the bond—and the later the maturity date, the larger the loss was if that bondholder sold the bond.

(Continued on page 146)

What Some People Lost When They Sold Their Municipal Bonds In 1984

TAX-EXEMPT BONDS				(July, 1984)
ISSUE	COUPON	MATURITY	PRICE	LOSS
	8 3/8%	'01	82 1/2	(17.5%)
	6 3/8%	'14	79	(21.0%)
	3 1/4%	'03	69	(31.0%)
	7 1/2%	'18	60	(40.0%)
	9 1/4%	'13	88	(12.0%)
	7 1/2%	'92	57 1/2	(42.5%)
	7 1/2%	'95	87 1/2	(12.5%)
	5 1/2%	'01	98 1/2	(01.5%)
	6 3/8%	'10	65 1/2	(34.5%)
	11 1/4%	'18	92	(08.0%)
	4.7 %	'06	67	(33.0%)
	4.3/4%	'03	54 1/2	(45.5%)
	9 1/4%	'20	82	(18.0%)
	10 1/4%	'20	92	(08.0%)
	9 1/2%	'12	83	(17.0%)
	5 1/2%	'07	57 1/2	(42.5%)
	6 %	'07	57	(43.0%)
	6 %	'15	14	(86.0%)
	7 %	'18	14 1/2	(85.5%)

What is best for you depends upon your circumstances. Turn the page to learn what your next steps could be. This secret is not investment advice, but it is a suggestion that you should think about your retirement savings regularly.

36

Tax free may not be as good as you think.

(Continued from page 144)

Naturally, if the bondholder did not sell the bond prior to maturity, the bondholder would get all of their money back assuming all is well with the municipality. Conversely, if interest rates were to decrease after one purchases a bond, the value of the bond would increase.

Next Steps

- Consult with your tax and legal advisors.

- Reach out to your insurance professional regarding products that can be taxable, tax-deferred, and tax free.

- If Municipal Bonds are being considered, ask your investment professional for examples of how increasing interest rates could decrease the value of your Municipal Bond if you had to sell it before maturity. Also ask how they can be insured, to what extent, and for sales literature about the insurance.

- Also ask if the Municipal Bonds are callable in the event that interest rates were to decrease.

- Circle back to your tax and legal advisors regarding the products that you are considering.

- Take cautious baby steps.

- Diversify.

- Understand the product that you are about to buy.

- Read what you are about to sign.

secret **37**

Retirement accounts are the worst place to turn for emergency money.

While Retirement Plans such as IRA's, 401(k) s, 403(b)s, and non-qualified annuities may be some of the best places to accumulate money since they accumulate tax deferred, they are the worst places to turn to for emergency money since withdrawals are taxable. Turn the page to learn where to get emergency money.

37

Retirement accounts are the worst place to turn to for emergency money.

Turning to your qualified money in your IRAs and in your 401(k) for emergency money is often not in your best interest. With the IRA, you can be hurt 3 ways. Firstly, any withdrawals of pre-taxed dollars from your IRA are taxable. Secondly, if you are younger than 59.5, there can also be a 10% federal tax penalty. For example, if you are age 50, and withdraw $10,000 from your IRA so you can get braces for your 3 kids, John, Mark, and Luke, you would pay anywhere from 15%-39% in federal income taxes, 4%-11% in state income taxes, and another 10% federal tax penalty. Said differently, you could lose up to 60% of that $10,000 IRA withdrawal in taxes. Thirdly, you would lose the power of those dollars remaining in your IRA and compounding interest on a tax-deferred basis for your retirement.

Some 401(k) plans have a loan provision., Admittedly, borrowing money from your 401(k) might be better than from your IRA since borrowing dollars from your 401(k) would not be a taxable event. It will still result in you having less money at retirement. Plus, your loan from your 401(k) becomes a taxable event if you do not repay it within 60 days of employment termination.

Is there an alternative? Turn to other places first for emergency money. On the opposite page, we give you a list of the best places to turn first for money. Naturally, turn to your money market or passbook savings accounts first since they will not trigger income taxes and they are less apt to have premature withdrawal penalties. Then turn to your CD at maturity. Need more money? Reluctantly, turn to your annuity for the insurer—not IRS—penalty-free 10% withdrawal. However, before you do, confirm with the insurer that there will be no surrender charges and that the withdrawal will not negatively impact future income from the Lifetime Income Rider you may have. Please see Secret 68.

Consider Withdrawing Money For Emergencies In This Order

1. Taxable Alternatives

   • Money Market

   • Passbook Savings

   • CD at Maturity

2. Non-Qualified Alternatives

   • Fixed Annuities

   • Variable Annuities

3. Qualified Money*

   • IRA

   • 401(k)**

   • Pension Plans

*Naturally, distributions must begin at age 70.5
**Some 410(k) plans have a loan provision.

Always consult with your advisors for the best place to withdraw your money since market conditions, tax law, and your particular situation could easily be different than the above.

What is best for you depends upon your circumstances. Turn the page to learn what your next steps could be. This secret is not investment advice, but it is a suggestion that you should think about your retirement savings regularly.

Retirement accounts are the worst place to turn to for emergency money.

Next Steps

- Consult with your tax and legal advisors.

- Reach out to your insurance professional regarding products that provide partial and total access to your money.

- Circle back to your tax and legal advisors regarding the products that you are considering.

- Take cautious baby steps.

- Diversify.

- Understand the product that you are about to buy.

- Read what you are about to sign.

Figure out without a pen or calculator how many years it will take for your money to double.

Insurance professionals are in the money business. You are not. Unfortunately, some insurance professionals talk a different language than you do. When they proudly talk about how their GMIBs and SPIAs can change your life, you hear Latin. Wouldn't it be nice if you could learn in 30 seconds something about money that took some financial professionals years to learn? Turn the page to discover how to calculate how money grows at any interest rate over any period of time without a pen or a calculator.

38 *Figure out without a pen or calculator how many years it will take for your money to double.*

The Rule of 72 calculates how many years it will take for money to double. You simply divide the interest rate into 72. If you were receiving 6% interest, then your money will double every 12 years (72 ÷ 6 = 12). Unfortunately, people often forget to take into account the income taxes that must be paid each year on the interest earned on their taxable money even if the interest is not withdrawn.

For example, you may be initially receiving 6% interest on some of your money, but 33% of that interest could be lost in federal and state income taxes. You're not getting 6% interest. You are getting 4%. Since you're getting 4% interest, your money will double every 18 years (72 ÷ 4 = 18). And, as you see on the chart on the following page, your $100,000 will be $200,000 in 18 years and $400,000 in 36 years.

However, look at what happens when we change how the 6% is taxed. Let's reposition some of your money to a tax–deferred alternative, an annuity, where taxes are paid later instead of now. Look at the difference. Your money can double every 12 years (72 ÷ 6 = 12)...$100,000 to $200,000 to $400,000 to $800,000.

Would you rather have $800,000 accumulating interest for you or $400,000 accumulating interest for you?

How Money Can Double

Rule of 72				
If you start with $100,000...				
Return	4%	6%	8%	12%
6 years				200K
12 years		200K		400K
18 years	200K		400K	800K
24 years		400K		1.6M
30 years				3.2M
36 years	400K	800K	1.6M	6.4M
42 years				12.8M
48 years		1.6M		25.6M
Doubles every...	18 years	12 years	9 years	6 years

The Rule of 72 is based on compounding a fixed rate of interest or return over a period of time. However, most investments do not provide a fixed rate and generate fluctuating returns. Therefore, the time in which an investment can double cannot be calculated with certainty. Also, tax-deferred annuities have fees and charges that should be compared to alternative investments that may be considered by the investor. This example does not include the fees and expenses associated with an annuity product. The above noted hypothetical example is for illustrative purposes only. It is not intended to represent or project any investment product.

38 *Figure out without a pen or calculator how many years it will take for your money to double.*

Next Steps
- Consult with your tax and legal advisors.
- Reach out to your insurance professional regarding products that can help you accumulate money on a tax-deferred basis.
- Circle back to your tax and legal advisors regarding the products that you are considering.
- Diversify.
- Determine your tolerance for risk and time horizon.
- Take cautious baby steps.

Reversing a ROTH Conversion could save you $160,000 or more.

W e promised that we would give you 2 times in which you could go back and reverse a financial mistake that you made. That's right, you can almost just wiggle your nose like Samantha did on the 1960's TV show *Bewitched*, and you can correct, reverse, and rewind a mistake that you may have made regarding your IRA and ROTH Conversion. The IRS calls it Recharacterization. You will call it priceless.

39

Reversing a ROTH Conversion could save you $160,000 or more.

A s you can see on the following page, the publication in which Recharacterization, in other words, do-overs, are discussed is Instructions Form 8606. In summary, you can change your mind if you converted your Traditional IRA to a ROTH IRA, converted your IRA to a ROTH IRA, or converted your ROTH IRA to a Traditional IRA.

Can you change your mind on all matters relating to IRAs and ROTH IRAs? No, and one example of no would be transferring employer contributions in a SEP IRA or SIMPLE IRA into a ROTH IRA. As always, consult with your tax advisor since so much is at stake.

Why would anyone want to change their minds? First, we all make mistakes. Secondly, relationships in marriages do change as well as how you file your tax return. The Recharacterization example that can potentially deliver the biggest tax savings is following a ROTH Conversion.

Let's assume that a hypothetical individual, named Jack, had decided to do a ROTH Conversion on February 1st in order to convert taxable income in the future to tax-free income for the future. Let's further assume that he had $1,000,000 in his IRA before the ROTH Conversion and that the income tax as a result of the ROTH Conversion was $400,000. As bad luck would have it, history began to repeat itself and the market behaves like it did in 2008 and Jack watches his account lose 40% in value. In other words, his account is worth $600,000 not the $1,000,000 it was worth when he did the ROTH Conversion. Jack's wife, Jill, was heard saying, "Jack, if we only had waited and converted to a ROTH now, we could have saved $160,000 in income taxes since paying taxes on $600,000 is a lot better than paying income taxes on $1,000,000."

(Continued on page 158)

Review This Document With Your Tax Advisor

Form **8606**	**Nondeductible IRAs**	OMB No. 1545-0074
Department of the Treasury Internal Revenue Service (99)	▶ Information about Form 8606 and its separate instructions is at *www.irs.gov/form8606.* ▶ Attach to Form 1040, Form 1040A, or Form 1040NR.	20**13** Attachment Sequence No. **48**

Name. If married, file a separate form for each spouse required to file Form 8606. See instructions.　　Your social security number

Fill in Your Address Only If You Are Filing This Form by Itself and Not With Your Tax Return ▶

Home address (number and street, or P.O. box if mail is not delivered to your home)	Apt. no.
City, town or post office, state, and ZIP code. If you have a foreign address, also complete the spaces below (see instructions).	

Foreign country name	Foreign province/state/county	Foreign postal code

Part I	**Nondeductible Contributions to Traditional IRAs and Distributions From Traditional, SEP, and SIMPLE IRAs**

Complete this part only if one or more of the following apply.
- You made nondeductible contributions to a traditional IRA for 2013.
- You took distributions from a traditional, SEP, or SIMPLE IRA in 2013 **and** you made nondeductible contributions to a traditional IRA in 2013 or an earlier year. For this purpose, a distribution does not include a rollover, qualified charitable distributions, one-time distribution to fund an HSA, conversion, recharacterization, or return of certain contributions.
- You converted part, but not all, of your traditional, SEP, and SIMPLE IRAs to Roth IRAs in 2013 (excluding any portion you recharacterized) **and** you made nondeductible contributions to a traditional IRA in 2013 or an earlier year.

1	Enter your nondeductible contributions to traditional IRAs for 2013, including those made for 2013 from January 1, 2014, through April 15, 2014 (see instructions)	1	
2	Enter your total basis in traditional IRAs (see instructions)	2	
3	Add lines 1 and 2	3	

In 2013, did you take a distribution from traditional, SEP, or SIMPLE IRAs, or make a Roth IRA conversion?　—— No ——▶ Enter the amount from line 3 on line 14.

4	Enter those contributions included on line
5	Subtract line 4 from line 3 . . . .
6	Enter the value of **all** your traditional, December 31, 2013, plus any outstanding
7	Enter your distributions from tradition 2013. **Do not** include rollovers, qualifie time distribution to fund an HSA, con returned contributions, or recharac contributions (see instructions) . . .
8	Enter the net amount you converted fr IRAs to Roth IRAs in 2013. **Do not** inc later recharacterized (see instructions). A
9	Add lines 6, 7, and 8 . . . . . .
10	Divide line 5 by line 9. Enter the result 3 places. If the result is 1.000 or more,
11	Multiply line 8 by line 10. This is the n you converted to Roth IRAs. Also enter
12	Multiply line 7 by line 10. This is t distributions that you did not convert to
13	Add lines 11 and 12. This is the nontax
14	Subtract line 13 from line 3. This is **you**
15	**Taxable amount.** Subtract line 12 fro 1040, line 15b; Form 1040A, line 11b; Note. You may be subject to an addit age 59½ at the time of the distribution

For Privacy Act and Paperwork Reduction Act N

> **Example.** You are married filing jointly and converted $20,000 from your traditional IRA to a new Roth IRA on May 20, 2011. On April 7, 2012, you decide to recharacterize the conversion. The value of the Roth IRA on that date is $19,000. You recharacterize the conversion by transferring that entire amount to a traditional IRA in a trustee-to-trustee transfer. You report $20,000 on Form 1040, line 15a. You do not include the $19,000 on line 15a because it did not occur in 2011 (you also do not report that amount on your 2012 return because it does not apply to the 2012 tax year). You attach a statement to Form 1040 explaining that (a) you made a conversion of $20,000 from a traditional IRA on May 20, 2011, and (b) you recharacterized the entire amount, which was then valued at $19,000, back to a traditional IRA on April 7, 2012.

39
Reversing a ROTH Conversion could save you $160,000 or more.

(Continued from page 156)

As good luck would have it, Jack remembered reading something in our book about "do-overs," "erasing mistakes," and "rewinding" back into the future. Jack ran to his bookshelf, quickly grabbed *75 Secrets*, rushed to the Index section, looked for do-overs, found the page number, and called his tax advisor.

Jack and Jill's tax advisor said that if they acted in time, they could erase, in other words, recharacterize, the conversion as if it never happened. They could also—assuming they follow the restrictions[1]—do another ROTH Conversion, pay $240,000 in income taxes instead of $400,000. Their tax advisor also reminded Jack and Jill that if history does repeat itself and the market goes up and their $600,000 returns to $1,000,000, they will pay no income taxes on the $400,000 gain and no income taxes on any income withdrawn by themselves or by their children from their $1,000,000 account since they did a ROTH Conversion.

Upon hearing that, Jill, looked at Jack and said," I am so glad I married you." And, that made Jack's day.

Next Steps

- Consult with your tax and legal advisors.
- Diversify.
- Act cautiously but read and understand before you sign.
- Circle back to your tax and legal advisors before buying any product that you are considering.
- IMPORTANT NOT: 401(k)s converted to ROTH 401(k)s cannot be recharacterized.

---

[1] *"You cannot convert and reconvert an amount during the same tax year or, if later, during the 30-day period following a recharacterization. If you reconvert during either of these periods, it will be a failed conversion".*
Source: Instruction form 8606, page 29.

There is an easy way to compute what your advisors are worth to you.

Are you getting your money's worth from your tax and legal advisors, insurance professional, and investment professional? Allow me to ask you two questions. In the past, how have they helped you? What makes some of your advisors and professionals special? To learn how to calculate their value, just turn the page.

40 *There is an easy way to compute what your advisors are worth to you.*

Since The Employee Benefit Research Institute reported that 50% of working Americans have $50,000 or less saved and 25% of them have nothing saved, the consumer needs an insurance professional now more than ever before.

How do we define an investment professional and an insurance professional? One can offer securities and insurance and the other can offer insurance. Having both investment and insurance professionals on your side makes common sense for many consumers.

However, this secret addresses the importance of working with a professional. There are several ways of defining a professional. Some sales people, not professionals, measure success by how much money they made that day. Too often that short-sightedness delivers too many one year relationships with clients and too few referrals.

On the other hand, professionals measure success in long-term relationships, so while "a lost sale" is still disappointing to them, "a lost sale" due to providing full disclosure or the disadvantages with the product being discussed is part of building a successful career.

In addition, professionals listen more than talk, care about the consumer more than themselves, tell a story of diversification, and remain balanced and fair by sharing the advantages and disadvantages of each product and rider.

Has your insurance professional helped you:
- Protect the people that you love with life insurance,
- Insure the assets you care about,
- Pay yourself first every month via saving or investing,
- Understand the advantages and disadvantages of each product,
- Diversify,
- Understand your tolerance for risk, your time horizon,
- Get a product that is 100 % suitable for you.

If so, they could be worth a great deal to you.

What An Insurance and/or Investment Professional Can Help You Do:

- Protect the people you love

- Insure the assets that are important to you

- Pay yourself first every week or month

- Understand the advantages/disadvantages

- Diversify

- Understand your tolerance for risk and your time horizon

What is best for you depends upon your circumstances. Turn the page to learn what your next steps could be. This secret is not investment advice, but it is a suggestion that you should think about your retirement savings regularly.

There is an easy way to compute what your advisors are worth to you.

Next Steps

- If you already have special tax and legal advisors and insurance professionals:

    Reach out to them.

    Meet them together at least once a year.

    Tell them what you want.

- If you do not have special tax and legal advisors and insurance professionals:

    Ask your friends and/or neighbors who is taking great care of them.

    Reflect on who took or is taking great care of your parent's insurance and investments.

    Consider meeting some of the professionals who call you at a nearby coffee shop.

secret **41**

You can make a tax-deductible contribution of $52,000 if you own a business.

Millions and millions of small business owners are not aware that they can slash their federal income taxes, build a large tax-deferred retirement account for themselves, and exclude some or all of their employees. Turn the page to learn one of the best kept secrets in retirement planning.

41

You can make a tax-deductible contribution of $52,000 if you own a business.

_____

T he Simplified Employee Pension Plan, (SEP), is another way that you can accumulate a great deal of money on a before tax basis, hence, slash income taxes. A SEP is an employer's sponsored retirement plan. A SEP can be used by almost any business, whether a corporation, partnership, or sole proprietor. Even an owner of a small business without any employees can have his/her own SEP. The SEP is sometimes called very special because it allows contributions by an employer of 25% of any employee's compensation up to $260,000* (subject to future cost–of–living adjustments) per year per employee or $52,000, whichever is less.

Must the employer cover all employees? Yes and no! An employer cannot discriminate, but there are conditions in which employees can be excluded. For example, if you are a small business owner, look around your shop, office, or store. Do you see any employees who are younger than 21? They can be excluded. Do you see any employees who will not work for you for 3 years? They too can be excluded, but they must become part of the plan in year 4 if they are still working with you.

Here are some of the SEP Benefits:

1. Less paperwork.
2. No expense for actuarial certification.
3. No expensive fees to draft a plan.
4. No special reporting requirements.
5. No fixed contribution requirement each year.
6. Some employees can be excluded indiscriminately.

The above are for employer contributions. If the SEP allows for employee contributions to personal IRA accounts, the personal contribution limit in 2014 is $5,500, or $6,500 if employee is 50 and older.

Benefits Of A Simplified Employee Pension Plan

- Reduce taxable income by as much as $52,000

- Less paperwork

- No expense for actuarial certification

- No expensive fees

- No special reporting

- No fixed contribution required each year

- Some employees can be excluded indiscriminately

Source: http://IRS.gov;W.V.H., Inc.

W.V.H., Inc., its employees, officers, directors are not qualified to provide tax or legal advice.

You can make a tax-deductible contribution of $52,000 if you own a business.

Next Steps
- Ask the IRS for their brochure about SEPs, 5305-SEP.
- Consult with your tax and legal advisors.
- Reach out to your insurance and/or investment professional for products that can be part of your SEP.
- Circle back to your tax and legal advisors regarding the products that you are considering.
- Take cautious baby steps.
- Diversify.
- Understand the product that you are about to buy.
- Read what you are about to sign.

secret 42

Time can be a friend or an enemy. Learn how to make it a friend.

The quality of your retirement depends on a number of variables. Sadly, some of the variables are variables that you cannot control such as what the market does, what kind of interest rates you get over the long term, tax changes, and inflation. However, when you start saving is something you can control. Turn the page to see if you have enough time.

Time can be a friend or an enemy. Learn how to make it a friend.

W hen you start saving and how much you save are often variables that you can control. While you may not like what you are about to see on the opposite page, time can be your friend or time can be your enemy.

Since the opposite page shows you how to accumulate $1,000,000 before taxes, you can use this chart for any goal you may have. Want to accumulate more? Simply double the amount you need to save. Want to accumulate less? Just save less.

Is it too late? While it may be too late to accumulate $1,000,000, it is not too late to accumulate money. Should you bother to start now? Absolutely! Your decision to begin saving today versus ignoring this problem of yours will affect how you live, where you live, and with whom you live. "After all, it is your life."

How Much Do You Need To Begin Saving Now To Have $1,000,000 Later?

Time can be a friend

$8,174 a year for 30 years at 8%

$17,144 a year for 30 years at 4%

$34,101 a year for 15 years at 8%

$48,020 a year for 15 years at 4%

Time can be an enemy

$157,830 a year for 5 years at 8%

$177,526 a year for 5 years at 4%

$285,216 a year for 3 years at 8%

$308,027 a year for 3 years at 4%

The above is hypothetical. Interest rates and returns do not stay level for long periods of time. Some products have fees, expenses, and risks. As a result, losses are possible with some products. This secret is not intended to provide investment advice, but it is a suggestion that you should think about your retirement savings regularly. Turn the page to learn what your next steps could be.

42 *Time can be a friend or an enemy. Learn how to make it a friend.*

Next Steps

- Consult with your tax and legal advisors.
- Reach out to your insurance professional for products that can potentially accumulate more money for you.
- Diversify.
- Ask questions.
- Take cautious baby steps.
- Verbalize with your advisors and insurance professional about your tolerance for risk, time horizon, wants, and needs.
- Keep 6 months' of income or more in highly liquid FDIC insured bank accounts.

Lock in a lifetime income stream at today's low interest rates.

*T*his secret was written by Scott Stolz, Senior Vice President, Private Client Group Investment Products, Raymond James Insurance Group; the views expressed in this secret are solely Scott's views and not necessarily the views of his company.

Financial advisors are increasingly recommending the use of an immediate annuity as vital piece of a comprehensive retirement income plan. While retirees have always intuitively understood the importance of receiving a steady check guaranteed for life (just ask anyone receiving a pension), most financial advisors have been slow to embrace this concept.

43

Lock in a lifetime income stream at today's low interest rates.

How difficult can it be to structure a portfolio to provide lifetime income? When the financial crisis hit, and many advisors—and their clients—realized guaranteeing an income for life was not as easy as they thought. The truth of the matter is that any retirement income portfolio that does not provide a guaranteed income for life must be invested relatively conservatively in order to reduce the chances that the next financial crises will have a crippling impact on your retirement income. By placing an immediate annuity in a retirement income plan to help cover your essential income needs, you can better position the rest of your portfolio for growth by investing it more aggressively. Perhaps more importantly, not having to worry about how your retirement income will be affected by the short term ups and downs of the stock and bond markets may allow you to sleep better at night.

Although I now see frequent articles about the benefits of an immediate annuity, these articles often come with a recommendation to wait until interest rates move back up. Since interest rates help determine the amount of income an immediate annuity will provide you, the basic premise behind the recommendation to wait is that it makes little sense to lock in a lifetime income stream at today's historically low interest rates. However, such advice is typically based on a lack of understanding of how immediate annuities are priced. You see, unlike CD's and bonds—both of which are priced based primarily on interest rates and maturity—a significant portion of the income you will receive from an immediate annuity is based on your life expectancy. In fact, the older you are, the greater the impact of your life expectancy relative to the current level of interest rates. Therefore, as interest rates have come down over the last 10 years, the amount of income paid on newly purchased immediate annuities has declined significantly less than other low risk investments that are often used for retirement income. Consider the following table using the average of leading insurance companies.

	2005 3.9% Avg	2010 2.7% Avg	2013 0.91% Avg*	Change in 8 years
5 Year Bank CD	$775,194	$1,127,820	$3,283,000	324%
Lifetime Income Annuity (Average of leading insurance companies)	$450,000	$457,000	$563,000	25%

Example: Male age 65, needing $30,000/year income - 20 Year Period Certain and Life. (payable in monthly installments)

*At the end of the CD maturity term, the full investment of the CD is returned whereas with annuities, the payout is represented by principal and interest.

5 year CD average on Bankrate.com of .91% as of January 15, 2013

Just 7 years ago, you would have had to put $775,194 into a 5 year certificate of deposit to generate $30,000 a year. Today, due to historically low interest rates, it would take over $3,283,000 to generate that same $30,000 income. By comparison, in 2005, a 65 year old male would have had to put $450,000 into an immediate annuity to guarantee $30,000 a year for life with the additional promise of paying the purchaser's beneficiary a lump sum equal to the difference between the $450,000 and the total payments made should the purchaser die prematurely (cash refund option).

Today, due to lower interest rates, it would indeed take more money to duplicate that same level of income. However, since a major portion of the pricing of the annuity is based on life expectancy, it would only take 25% more.

43

Lock in a lifetime income stream at today's low interest rates.

Critics of this approach would be quick to point out that I'm comparing apples to oranges with this example. And to an extent, they would be right. The CD is providing the $30,000 in income solely from the interest earned on the CD. When the CD matures in 5 years, the $3,283,000 would still be intact. This is not the case with the annuity since it is returning your principal and interest to you over your lifetime. Once the annuity has paid out paid out 20 years in payments, the only thing you are entitled to receive is the $30,000 in annual income for as long as you live. However, his criticism assumes that these two choices are both available to you. If you need $30,000 in annual income and you don't have 3.28 million dollars, you are going to be spending both your principal and interest no matter what approach you take. Therefore, the goal is to generate the income as efficiently as possible.

And yes, you could wait until interest rates go back up. When this occurs you will get more income from the annuity. Plus, you would have the added advantage of being older, thereby giving you more income due to your life expectancy. However, I've heard people recommending to wait until "interest rates go back up" for 20 years now. Eventually, those suggesting you wait will prove to be right. The only question is can you wait that long?

Next Steps

- Consult with your tax and legal advisors.
- Understand what you are buying
- Diversify

secret

There are five big advantages and three disadvantages that annuities have over CDs.

W hile no one should put all or most of their money into annuities or into any other product for that matter, annuities can be a great alternative for some of your money since they offer five unique benefits. If you turn the page, you will discover the five reasons why annuities deserve your consideration when planning for retirement.

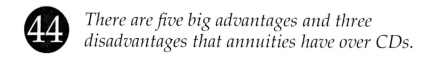

44 *There are five big advantages and three disadvantages that annuities have over CDs.*

5 Advantages

1. You can pay less income taxes. With the money in taxable alternatives such as Certificates of Deposit, you must pay income taxes on the earnings regardless of whether you leave the earnings in or take the earnings out. With the annuity, you pay income taxes when you want to, when you take the earnings out.

You can potentially have more money with an annuity than with a taxable alternative.

2. You can potentially have more money with an annuity than with a taxable alternative. This can occur because earnings accumulate three ways inside of an annuity. Earnings compound on top of premium, earnings compound on top of earnings, and, earnings compound on top of the dollars that you normally send to the government in income taxes.

3. You can have four ways to withdraw your money. 1) You can take 10% of your annuity value out each year, 2) You can surrender your annuity. And, if you do so during the surrender charge period, there are surrender charges and a possible market value adjustment, 3) You can elect monthly income and receive guaranteed monthly income for any number of years or for life and, 4) You can put the Guaranteed Minimum Withdrawal Benefit rider in motion and receive, conceptually, 5% of your Income Benefit Base every year for life assuming that your annuity has this rider.

4. You can enjoy the tax advantages that the government has extended to non-qualified annuities. You could say that your annuity picks up from where your existing IRA leaves off because just like your IRA, earnings accumulate without current taxes. Income taxes are paid when interest is withdrawn. And, there is a 10% excise tax penalty if dollars are withdrawn prior to age 59.5. However, unlike the IRA, there is no maximum on how much money you can put into your non-qualified annuity and you don't have to begin taking dollars out at the age of 70.5.

(Continued on page 178)

The Major Differences Between CDs And Annuities

1. Potentially more money

2. Less current taxes

3. Easy Access

4. IRA Companion

5. Earnings

All parties should see the insurer disclosure and annuity contract for guaranteed interest rates and values. Bank CDs are insured up to applicable limits by the FDIC. Annuities are insurance products and are NOT insured by the FDIC or any other federal government agency. The guarantees in an annuity contract are subject to the claims-paying ability of the insurer making the guarantees. Annuities have earnings which are taxable upon withdrawal and, if taken before age 59.5, may be subject to IRS penalties. Withdrawals taken during the Surrender Charge period above the penalty-free amount will be subject to Surrender Charges and a possible Market Value Adjustment.

44

There are five big advantages and three disadvantages that annuities have over CDs.

(Continued from page 176)

5. You can select how your earnings could potentially accumulate since you can receive an interest rate guaranteed for one year or more, or your earnings can be based on the changes in an external index like The Dow Jones Industrial Average^{SM}, or your earnings can potentially accumulate based on an investment portfolio professionally managed (Variable Annuity).

Would you like to reduce the amount of income taxes you pay on your bank interest?

The key question is, "Would you like to reduce the amount of income taxes you pay on your bank interest?"

3 Disadvantages

1. Bank CDs are insured up to applicable limits by the FDIC. Annuities are insurance products and are *not* insured by the FDIC or any other federal government agency. However, the guarantees in an annuity contract are subject to the claims paying ability of the insurer making the guarantees.
2. Annuities have earnings, which are taxable upon withdrawal and if taken before age 59.5, may be subject to IRS penalties.
3. Withdrawals taken during the Surrender Charge period above the penalty-free amount will be subject to Surrender Charges and a possible Market Value Adjustment.

Assuming that a) you keep 6 months' income or more in highly liquid short-term FDIC insured accounts and b) you select a respected, highly rated insurer to issue the annuity, do you and your tax and legal advisors think that the five annuity advantages outweigh the three annuity disadvantages for some of your money?

Next Steps

*   Consult with your tax and legal advisors.
*   Reach out to your insurance professional regarding products that can help you save for your retirement.
*   Take cautious baby steps.

There are 5 risks potentially more devastating than risk to principal.

Although many people focus solely on risk to principal, there are five other risks that can have a devastating effect on your retirement. Turn the page to discover how crippling inflation, income taxes, the lack of diversification, living too long, and changes to Social Security can be.

45 *There are 5 risks potentially more devastating than risk to principal.*

1. Inflation: Since 1950, inflation has averaged slightly over 4%. If that were to continue, a dollar today would purchase only 60 cents worth of goods and services in 10 short years.

2. Income Taxes: You may think that you have been getting 6% interest on some of your money, but if you are in a combined tax bracket of 33%, you are really only getting 4% interest since part of your interest has been lost to income taxes every year. You could survive on 4% if there were 0% inflation, but a historical annual inflation rate of slightly over 4% since 1950 means that you have been going backwards.

3. Lack of Diversification: We all know that we should never put all of our eggs in one basket, but we still do. You should diversify. Spread out your dollars among different alternatives. If you do diversify, you are less apt to be seriously affected if interest rates, returns, and inflation go in the wrong direction.

4. Living Longer Than Expected: In the 1940s, the average male lived to age 62. In 1940, the Census Bureau reported that there were less than 4,000 people age 100 or older. The Census Bureau now reports that there are over 53,000 people age 100 or older. The only unfortunate thing about longer life expectancy is outliving your money. In the past, you had 45 years to work and save money for a comfortable 10-year retirement. Now, you have those same 45 years to work and save money, but you need money for 20 and 30 years of retirement, not 10 years.

(Continued on page 182)

The 5 Most Overlooked Risks

1. Inflation

2. Income Taxes

3. Lack of Diversification

4. Living Longer

5. Social Security

Sources: Bureau of Labor Statistics; Census Bureau; W.V.H., Inc.

What is best for you depends upon your circumstances. Turn the page to learn what your next steps could be. This secret is not investment advice, but it is a suggestion that you should think about your retirement savings regularly.

45 *There are 5 risks potentially more devastating than risk to principal.*

(Continued from page 180)

5. Social Security: Since 1935, the Social Security program has allowed employees and employers to set aside dollars so that they can retire in dignity. Will Social Security change? Will it disappear? No one currently knows those answers, but everyone knows that they should control their own destiny. We must stop depending upon the government. We must learn how to overcome inflation, reduce current income taxes, diversify, and plan for the future by thinking about our money regularly. We, and no one else, should control our own retirement.

Would you now like to take a step toward being more financially independent?

Summary:

Owning an annuity can address each of these 5 risks.

1. Inflation since you can have potentially more money later.

2. Income taxes since you can pay taxes later.

3. Diversifying since an annuity can be one of many products in your portfolio.

4. Guaranteed monthly income since annuitization or withdrawals can give you income for as long as you live.

5. A supplement to Social Security since an annuity can be an added source of money during retirement.

Next Steps

• Consult with your tax and legal advisors.

• Reach out to your insurance professional regarding products that can help you overcome these 5 risks.

• Circle back to your tax and legal advisors regarding the products that you are considering.

• Take cautious baby steps.

• Diversify.

secret **46**

An annuity can lower both your AGI & tax bracket, then get you new tax deductions.

Accountants call it the "tipping point." It is when your taxable income reaches a lower level (tipping point) and previously disallowed deductions "tip over" and suddenly become allowed deductions. As a result, your income taxes are reduced! Would you like to learn how to reduce your effective tax rate by over 33%? If so, turn the page and learn how to get new deductions, reduce your tax bracket, and your tax liability?

46

An annuity can lower both your AGI & tax bracket, then get you new tax deductions.

On the opposite page, we have a hypothetical couple, Ward and June with 2 young kids, Wally and Beaver. Ward makes $120,000 a year. June stays at home, pays tuition of $5,000 to attend a near-by college, and helps out with the small rental property that Ward and June just bought. Ward participates in his company's retirement plan at work, June has an IRA, and they earn $25,000 in taxable interest from money they have in the bank.

As good fortune would have it, Ward and June bought our book *75 Secrets* and decided to consult with their tax advisor, reach out to their insurance professional, and meet both of them at the same time. At that meeting, the visual on the opposite page was shown to them. As you can see, if they keep things the same, their adjusted gross income (AGI) remains at $135,500, $97,200 after the deductions they always take, with a tax liability of $22,149, very similar to last year's tax liability.

However, look at what happens when they change how the $25,000 in bank interest is taxed. By simply repositioning the money they have in the bank into tax-deferred alternatives, suddenly Ward and June's adjusted gross income (AGI) "tips over" and decreases to $56,450, their tax liability plummets from $22,149 to only $8,398 since they can now get a $15,000 deduction on their rental property, a deduction on part of Ward's IRA contribution, almost all of June's tuition is now deductible, and, of course, the $25,000 of interest is not taxable until they withdraw the interest. When Ward and June are done dancing around the table, Jim Anderson, the insurance agent reminds Ward and June about taking cautious baby steps and repositioning only some of their bank money into a tax-deferred alternative.

Do you want to see if you can "tip over" your adjusted gross income, get new tax deductions, and reduce income taxes? If so, your Next Steps are on the next page.

Before And After Annuity Comparison

	Before	After	Change
Wages	$120,000	$120,000	$ -
Interest	25,000	-	(25,000)
Rental Losses	(2,500)	(15,000)	(12,500)
IRA - Husband	-	(1,250)	(1,250)
IRA - Wife	(5,000)	(5,000)	-
Tuition Deduction	(2,000)	(4,000)	(2,000)
Adjusted Gross Income	135,500	94,750	(40,750)
Mortgage Interest	(15,000)	(15,000)	-
Property Taxes	(3,000)	(3,000)	-
State Taxes	(4,000)	(4,000)	-
Contributions	(1,500)	(1,500)	-
Exemptions	(14,800)	(14,800)	-
Deductions	$(38,300)	(38,300)	-
Taxable Income	$97,200	$56,450	$40,750
Tax - Federal	$16,556	$7,211	$(8,935)
Tax - California	6,293	2,777	(3,516)
Child Tax Credit	(700)	(2,000)	(1,300)
Net Tax	$ 22,149	$ 8,398	$(13,751)
Effective Tax Rate	22.8%	14.9%	33.7%

What is best for you depends upon your circumstances. Turn the page to learn what your next steps could be. This secret is not investment advice, but it is a suggestion that you should think about your retirement savings regularly. W.V.H., Inc., its officers, and its employees are not trained or qualified to provide tax or legal advice.

All parties should see the insurer disclosure and annuity contract for guaranteed interest rates and values. Bank CDs are insured up to applicable limits by the FDIC. Annuities are insurance products and are NOT insured by the FDIC or any other federal government agency. The guarantees in an annuity contract are subject to the claims-paying ability of the insurer making the guarantees. Annuities have earnings which are taxable upon withdrawal and, if taken before age 59.5, may be subject to IRS penalties. Withdrawals taken during the Surrender Charge period above the penalty-free amount will be subject to Surrender Charges and a possible Market Value Adjustment.

The above chart is based upon 2013 tax deductions and tax brackets.

46 *An annuity can lower both your AGI & tax bracket, then get you new tax deductions.*

Next Steps

- Reach out to your tax advisor.

- See if lowering your taxable income will lower your adjusted gross income to a point that "tips" you into a lower tax bracket.

- Reach out to your insurance and/or investment professional to schedule a meeting between you and your tax advisor.

- Take cautious baby steps.

secret

Your $5,000 could have the purchasing power of $2,280 in 15 short years.

Tax deferral helps you potentially overcome the real effects of inflation, less purchasing power, since it potentially helps you accumulate more money. And, more money later can help you buy more expensive things later. If you do not want to buy candy bars 50% smaller or go to Hoboken, New Jersey for 2 weeks instead of Paris, France, then please turn the page to learn how to potentially maintain your current purchasing power.

47 *Your $5,000 could have the purchasing power of $2,280 in 15 short years.*

Let's assume that you are earning $5,000 in taxable interest each year and you are in a 28% tax bracket. If that is the case, $1,400 of the $5,000 disappears in income taxes. The balance, $3,600, remains with you. However, if we have a 3% rate of inflation each year, your purchasing power quickly erodes year after year after year.

On the opposite page, we show how quickly your purchasing power can erode.

After 7 short years, assuming a 3% inflation rate, your initial $3,600 in after-tax interest will have the purchasing power of $2,909. After 15 years, your purchasing power will have eroded to $2,280.

If you are currently earning taxable interest from the bank and you think that 3% inflation is possible, what are you doing about this problem of yours?

You can either ignore this problem and purchase less and less as time goes on or you can sit down with your tax and legal advisors and then your insurance and/or investment professional and get your dollars to work harder and smarter.

Would you agree that the more money you have later, the more purchasing power you will have later?

If so, consider putting some of your money in products that can accumulate tax deferred just in case there is inflation.

How your Purchasing Power Decreases Because of Inflation

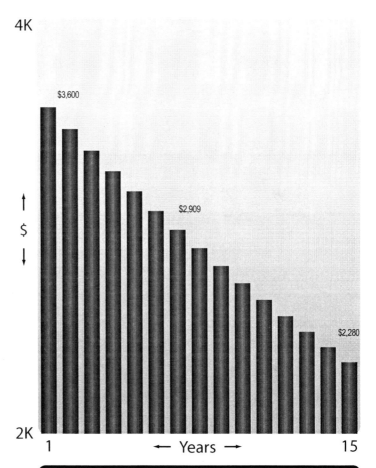

Assumptions: 3% inflation; 28% federal tax bracket

What is best for you depends upon your circumstances. Turn the page to learn what your next steps could be. This secret is not investment advice, but it is a suggestion that you should think about your retirement savings regularly.

Your $5,000 could have the purchasing power of $2,280 in 15 short years.

Next Steps

- Consult with your tax and legal advisors.
- Reach out to your insurance professional to lessen the impact of inflation.
- Circle back to your tax and legal advisors regarding the products that you are considering.
- Read what you sign.
- Diversify.
- Take cautious baby steps but act if it is in your best interest.

secret 48

Thinking about buying a product for too long can cost you a lot of money.

While rushing into a buying decision is unwise, thinking and thinking about buying a financial product can cost you a lot of money. Fortunately, one way to calculate the cost of waiting is only one page away.

48 *Thinking about buying a product for too long can cost you a lot of money.*

T he cost of indecision. How much does it cost when you postpone making a wise decision? On the opposite page, we compare the accumulation between a taxable alternative like a CD to a tax-deferred alternative like an annuity but from a different dimension. This time we are "not" showing how many extra dollars you can have with an annuity. We are showing you the cost if you stay where you are, in other words, if you keep the dollars in the taxable alternative instead of the tax-deferred annuity. Your cost for procrastinating. Your cost for not following the advice of your tax and legal advisors and the suggestions of your insurance and/or investment professional. As you will see on the opposite page, when you simply subtract the value of a taxable alternative from the annuity value, the result can be your cost of waiting instead of acting.

Comparing a Taxable Alternative
To A Tax-Deferred Alternative

	Taxable Alternative	Tax-Deferred Alternative	
Year	Accumulation Value	Accumulation Value	The Cost
1	102,880	104,000	1,120
5	115,254	121,665	6,411
10	132,834	148,024	15,190
15	153,096	180,094	26,998
20	176,449	219,112	42,663
25	203,364	266,584	63,230
30	234,384	324,340	89,956

Assumes $100,000 premium, 4% interest,
28% tax bracket

All parties should see the insurer disclosure and annuity contract for guaranteed interest rates and values. Bank CDs are insured up to applicable limits by the FDIC. Annuities are NOT insured by the FDIC or any other agency and are subject to investment risks, including the possible loss of principal. The guarantees in an annuity contract are subject to the claims-paying ability of the insurer making the guarantees. Annuities have earnings which are taxable upon withdrawal and, if taken before age 59.5, may be subject to a 10% Federal early withdrawal penalty. Annuities can have a surrender charge period of 10 years or more and a possible Market Value Adjustment. Naturally, the above charts are hypothetical, and the charts do not represent any specific investment or insurance product.

Thinking about buying a product for too long can cost you a lot of money.

Next Steps

- Consult with your tax and legal advisors.

- Reach out to your insurance and/or investment professional. Understand the annuity(ies) that you are considering by reading the insurance company literature, specimen annuity contract; and the prospectus if considering a Variable Annuity.

- Diversify.

- Act cautiously by asking questions and take cautious baby steps.

- Verbalize with your tax and legal advisors and your insurance and/or investment professional about your tolerance for risk, time horizon, wants and needs.

- Keep 6 months' of income or more in highly liquid FDIC insured bank accounts.

You can select the best type of annuity if you diversify.

Would you like to know a secret? It is almost impossible to select the best type of annuity since every type of annuity performs differently during the renewal years. However, it is possible to improve the probability of you getting the best type of annuity for some of your money and guarantee that all of your money does not go in the wrong type of annuity. If you turn the page, you will discover why diversification plays an important role in making the right decision.

You can select the best type of annuity if you diversify.

You can improve the probability of getting the best and second best type of annuity for a lot of your money. And, you can make sure that all of your money does not go into the wrong type of annuity.

How? Simply diversify your money among the 3 or 4 types of annuities:

- 3 types of annuities if you have zero tolerance for risk
- 4 types of annuities if you have some tolerance for risk

On the opposite page, we show how 4 hypothetical annuities might behave during a Bull and Bear Market. As you can see, different types of annuities can behave differently based on factors that are not known at the time of purchase.

A solution to consider: diversify your retirement dollars among 3 or 4 types of annuities so that 50% or more of your money will be in the 2 best types of annuities and that all of your money will *never* be in the wrong annuity.

What are the 4 types:

- Indexed Annuities: Gains can be calculated by crediting interest based on a percentage of the gains in an external index like The Dow Jones Industrial Average[SM].

- Multi-Year Guarantee Annuity: Interest rate guarantees of 1-10 years.

- Traditional: One year interest rate guarantee with renewal interest rates declared by insurer.

- Variable: designed to potentially perform over the long term better than the above 3 types of Fixed Annuities; however, there is the risk to losing part of your premium due to market risk.

How 4 Types Of Annuities Can Behave

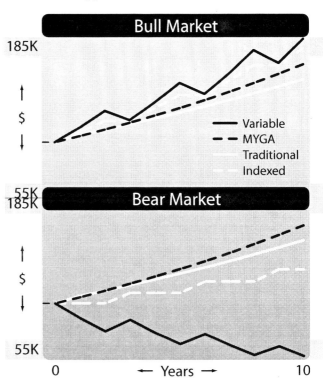

Bull Market

185K

↑
$
↓

— Variable
- - - MYGA
Traditional
Indexed

55K
Bear Market
185K

↑
$
↓

55K

0 ← Years → 10

Assumptions:
 Premium of $100,000
  Bull Market
    Variable Annuity: A gross portfolio return of 12% in years 1, 2, 4,
                5, 7, 8, 10; 6% loss in years 3, 6, 9.
    Multi Year Guaranteed Annuity: 5% interest every year
    Traditional Annuity: 6% interest in year 1; 4% interest thereafter
    Indexed Annuity: 8.4% interest in years 1, 2, 4, 5, 7, 8, 10;
                0% interest in years 3, 6, 9.
                70% participation rate times 12% = 8.4%
  Bear Market
    Variable Annuity: 12% loss in years 1, 2, 4, 5, 7, 8, 10;
                A gross portfolio return of 12% in years 3, 6, 9.
    Multi Year Guaranteed Annuity: 5% interest every year
    Traditional Annuity: 6% interest in year 1; 4% interest thereafter
    Indexed Annuity: 0% interest in years 1, 2, 4, 5, 7, 8, 10;
                8.4% interest in years 3, 6, 9.
                (70% participation rate times 12% = 8.4%)

49 *You can select the best type of annuity if you diversify.*

Important Disclaimer:

The interest rates for the Tax-Deferred Fixed Annuity are hypothetical since interest rates vary by product and carrier. All parties should see the insurer disclosure and annuity contract for guaranteed interest rates and values. Bank CDs are insured up to applicable limits by the FDIC. Annuities are insurance products and are NOT insured by the FDIC or any other federal government agency. The guarantees in an annuity contract are subject to the claims-paying ability of the insurer making the guarantees. Annuities have earnings which are taxable upon withdrawal and, if taken before age 59.5 may be subject to IRS penalties. Withdrawals taken during the Surrender Charge period above the penalty-free amount will be subject to Surrender Charges and a possible Market Value Adjustment.

Next Steps

- Consult with your tax and legal advisors.

- Reach out to your insurance professionals and ask for the disadvantages and the advantages of the annuities they are recommending; since every annuity has disadvantages; you just want to make sure that in your individual circumstance, the advantages outweigh the disadvantages.

- Take cautious baby steps.

- Diversify

- Read and understand what you are about to sign.

secret **50**

Your annuity can avoid probate if you use the right words.

I t is common for heirs to lose thousands of dollars in probate costs, to be denied access to their dollars for months, and become embarrassed by the publicity that comes with dollars tied up in probate. On the next page, you'll learn how to avoid probate by using the right words.

50 *Your annuity can avoid probate if you use the right words.*

W hat is probate?

When a person dies, the Probate Court becomes involved to make sure the decedent's assets are divided among those persons legally entitled to it. If the decedent left a will, the division of assets will be carried out according to a will. If the decedent did not leave a will, the assets will be divided according to that state's "intestacy" laws. For example, $100,000 to the spouse, 50 % to the spouse and the balance to the children. If no children, the parents of the deceased can get the children's share.

The Probate Court will oversee the distribution of the estate (the assets) but will make sure that the debts of the decedent, funeral expenses, and taxes are paid before distributing the remaining assets of the estate. Arguably, probate has 3 major disadvantages: publicity, delay, and expense.

Publicity: What the decedent has in assets, liability and who gets the remaining assets will be part of the public record. Shortly, you will learn how to legally "hide"some assets from the public record.

Delay: It can take months for assets to get to your loved ones. Shortly, you will learn how to expedite assets going to your loved ones.

Expense: It's not uncommon for probate costs to be in the thousands of dollars. Shortly, you will learn how to bypass some of those probate expenses.

(Continued on page 202)

secret 50

4 Ways To Avoid Probate In Many States

1. Beneficiary designation for annuity and life contracts

2. Joint tenancy

3. Gift

4. Living trust

W.V.H., Inc., its employees, officers, directors are not qualified to provide tax or legal advice.

50 *Your annuity can avoid probate if you use the right words.*

(Continued from page 200)

In fact there are 4 ways to potentially avoid publicity, delay, and lessen the expense of Probate

1. The decedent owning an asset in joint tenancy

2. Gifting

3. Living Trusts

4. Beneficiary designations for annuity and life insurance contracts and—in some states—bank accounts where a beneficiary is named "in trust for ."

Next Steps

- Consult with your tax and legal advisors; confirm that annuities can avoid probate in your state if you name someone as the beneficiary. If so, ask for the recommended beneficiary wording.

- Reach out to your insurance professional and your bankers regarding products that can potentially avoid probate.

- Take cautious baby steps.

- Circle back to your tax and legal advisors regarding the products that you are considering buying.

- Diversify.

- Read and understand what you are about to sign.

- Consult an attorney who knows how probate works in your state. States can differ.

- Avoiding the publicity, expense, and delay of probate should not be the major reason for you wanting to own an annuity. However, if you want tax deferral, guarantees, the option to elect lifetime income, and the probate advantages discussed in this secret, then reach out to your insurance and/or investment professional.

You could be losing 32% of your bank interest every year. Maybe more!

More spendable income later is more likely if you start deferring income taxes now and accumulate money at a faster pace than inflation. As you will soon see, federal and state income taxes can take away 32 cents from every dollar of interest you earn in the bank. If you want to keep 100 cents earning interest for you instead of 68 cents earning interest for you, just turn the page.

51

You could be losing 32% of your bank interest every year. Maybe more!

O n the opposite page, we show what could be happening to the interest you now earn on taxable alternatives such as Certificates of Deposit, Money Market accounts, passbook savings, Treasury bills, and Treasury bonds.

"28 cents is going to Uncle Sam, and 4 cents is going to your state capitol (state income taxes). This leaves you with only 68 cents out of every dollar. What are you doing about this problem of yours?"

You can do nothing about it or you can sit down with an insurance or investment professional and they can help you reduce state and federal income taxes by repositioning some of your money from taxable alternatives to Tax-Deferred Annuities.

What Is Happening To Your Taxable Interest

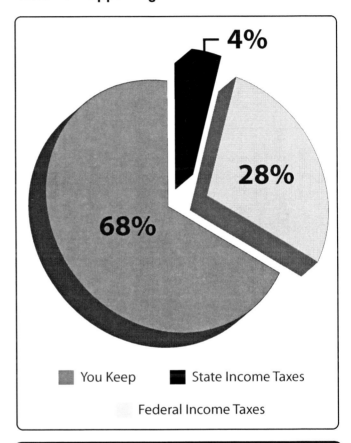

4%

28%

68%

■ You Keep   ■ State Income Taxes

Federal Income Taxes

What is best for you depends upon your circumstances. Turn the page to learn
what your next steps could be. This secret is not investment advice, but it is
a suggestion that you should think about your retirement savings regularly.

You could be losing 32% of your bank interest every year. Maybe more!

Next Steps

- Consult with your tax and legal advisors.

- Based upon the recommendation of your advisors, reach out to your insurance professional and/or investment professional for ways to reduce taxes on interest.

- Action begins with a decision, but act if it is in your best interest.

- Take cautious baby steps.

- Diversify.

- Read and understand what you are about to sign.

52

You should put some of your qualified money into an annuity.

Many critics have questioned the wisdom of putting qualified money into an annuity since qualified money accumulates tax deferred regardless of whether it is in CDs, Mutual Funds, etc. While they might be right that you should not put all of your qualified money into an annuity, the next page gives you 6 reasons why an annuity could make sense for some of your qualified money such as your IRA.

52 *You should put some of your qualified money into an annuity.*

Tax deferral is only one of the benefits to owning an annuity.

There are parties who feel that qualified money such as IRAs should not go into a tax-deferred annuity since they feel that the major benefit to owning an annuity is tax deferral. With qualified plans, you already get tax deferral. Fortunately for you, tax deferral is only one of the benefits of owning an annuity. In fact, there are at least six reasons for you to put some of your qualified money into an annuity.

1. An annuity is the only financial retirement vehicle that can guarantee monthly income to you for as long as you and your spouse live.

2. While all tax-deferred annuity policies allow you to "annuitize" the annuity value and, in return, get a guaranteed check for life, monthly, quarterly, or annually, some annuities also have a Lifetime Income rider that will allow you to a) receive lifetime income plus b) have access to your money if you or your heirs need more.

3. Interest rates with Fixed Annuities or the return with Variable Annuities might be higher than where your money is now.

4. It is possible that the annual fees and expenses with an annuity are either non-existent, low, or worth it when you take into account the guarantees specified in the annuity contract.

5. Speaking of guarantees, Fixed Annuities offer a guaranteed interest rate for the life of the annuity and some Variable Annuities offer other living benefit guarantees not found in other alternatives.

6. With many annuities, insurance company surrender charges disappear to 0% after the surrender charge period, unlike other financial products where penalties reappear when they are renewed.

The 6 Reasons To Put Qualified Money Into Annuities

1. Income

2. Rider*

3. Return

4. Fees

5. Lifetime Rate

6. Disappearing Charges

*With some Annuities

All parties should see the insurer disclosure and annuity contract for guaranteed interest rates and values. Bank CDs are insured up to applicable limits by the FDIC. Annuities are insurance products and are NOT insured by the FDIC or any other federal government agency. The guarantees in an annuity contract are subject to the claims-paying ability of the insurer making the guarantees. Annuities have earnings which are taxable upon withdrawal and, if taken before age 59.5, may be subject to IRS penalties. Withdrawals taken during the Surrender Charge period above the penalty-free amount will be subject to Surrender Charges and a possible Market Value Adjustment.

You should put some of your qualified money into an annuity.

Next Steps

- Consult with your tax and legal advisors.
- Based upon their recommendation, reach out to your insurance professional and/or investment professional.
- Action begins with a decision.
- Take cautious baby steps.
- Diversify.

You can reduce the income taxes that you are paying on your Social Security Income.

P eople can potentially reduce or eliminate the income taxes they are paying on their Social Security income by repositioning some of the money they have in the bank to a tax-deferred annuity. Turn the page if you want to see if you are paying taxes unnecessarily on your Social Security income.

You can reduce the income taxes that you are paying on your Social Security Income.

Why pay income taxes on interest you don't need yet?

In the worksheet on the next page, we give one example of a hypothetical couple age 65 who receives $12,000 in Social Security benefits (line 1). Line 3 represents $ 17,000 in income such as pension, capital gains, alimony, etc. and $17,000 in taxable interest as a result of interest earned on Certificates of Deposit, Passbook Savings, and Money Market Accounts. Line 4 shows $800 in Municipal Bond interest. As you can see on line 18, they are paying income taxes, perhaps, unnecessarily, on $4,400 of Social Security income.

Since this hypothetical couple did not need all of their taxable bank interest yet, they transferred some of the money they had in the bank into a tax-deferred annuity. Firstly, they transferred only some of their money since no one should put all or most of their money into any one product. Secondly, they chose a tax-deferred annuity over a taxable account since annuity interest credited and not withdrawn is not reported on this worksheet. For example, if the hypothetical couple decreased their bank taxable interest from $17,000 to $8,200, line 3 would then be $25,200 and line 19 would be zero. Would you like to potentially reduce or eliminate taxes on your Social Security income? If so, turn the page for more information.

Please go to pages 348 for a quick way to check if your benefits are taxable and page 349 to look at the IRS Worksheet without any added numbers. ALL PARTIES SHOULD REVIEW THIS IRS SOCIAL SECURITY WORKSHEET-LINES 20A AND 20B WITH THEIR TAX ADVISOR.

How Bank Interest Causes Social Security Income To Be Taxed

Social Security Benefits Worksheet—Lines 20a and 20b   *Keep for Your Records*

Before you begin:	✓ Complete Form 1040, lines 21 and 23 through 32, if they apply to you.
	✓ Figure any write-in adjustments to be entered on the dotted line next to line 36 (see the instructions for line 36).
	✓ If you are married filing separately and you lived apart from your spouse for all of 2013, enter "D" to the right of the word "benefits" on line 20a. If you do not, you may get a math error notice from the IRS.
	✓ Be sure you have read the **Exception** in the line 20a and 20b instructions to see if you can use this worksheet instead of a publication to find out if any of your benefits are taxable.

1. Enter the total amount from **box 5** of **all** your **Forms SSA-1099** and **Forms RRB-1099.** Also, enter this amount on Form 1040, line 20a .... **1.** __12,000__

2. Enter one-half of line 1 .... **2.** __6,000__

3. Combine the amounts from Form 1040, lines 7, 8a, 9a, 10 through 14, 15b, 16b, 17 through 19, and 21 .... **3.** __34,000__

4. Enter the amount, if any, from Form 1040, line 8b .... **4.** __800__

5. Combine lines 2, 3, and 4 .... **5.** __40,800__

6. Enter the total of the amounts from Form 1040, lines 23 through 32, plus any write-in adjustments you entered on the dotted line next to line 36 .... **6.** __0__

7. Is the amount on line 6 less than the amount on line 5?

   ☐ **No.** 🛑 None of your social security benefits are taxable. Enter -0- on Form 1040, line 20b.

   ☒ **Yes.** Subtract line 6 from line 5 .... **7.** __40,800__

8. If you are:
   - Married filing jointly, enter $32,000
   - Single, head of household, qualifying widow(er), or married filing separately and you **lived apart** from your spouse for all of 2013, enter $25,000
   - Married filing separately and you lived with your spouse at any time in 2013, skip lines 8 through 15; multiply line 7 by 85% (.85) and enter the result on line 16. Then go to line 17

   .... **8.** __32,000__

9. Is the amount on line 8 less than the amount on line 7?

   ☐ **No.** 🛑 None of your social security benefits are taxable. Enter -0- on Form 1040, line 20b. If you are married filing separately and you **lived apart** from your spouse for all of 2013, be sure you entered "D" to the right of the word "benefits" on line 20a.

   ☒ **Yes.** Subtract line 8 from line 7 .... **9.** __8,800__

10. Enter: $12,000 if married filing jointly; $9,000 if single, head of household, qualifying widow(er), or married filing separately and you **lived apart** from your spouse for all of 2013 .... **10.** __12,000__

11. Subtract line 10 from line 9. If zero or less, enter -0- .... **11.** __0__

12. Enter the **smaller** of line 9 or line 10 .... **12.** __8,800__

13. Enter one-half of line 12 .... **13.** __4,400__

14. Enter the **smaller** of line 2 or line 13 .... **14.** __4,400__

15. Multiply line 11 by 85% (.85). If line 11 is zero, enter -0- .... **15.** __0__

16. Add lines 14 and 15 .... **16.** __4,400__

17. Multiply line 1 by 85% (.85) .... **17.** __10,200__

18. **Taxable social security benefits.** Enter the **smaller** of line 16 or line 17. Also enter this amount on Form 1040, line 20b .... **18.** __4,400__

TIP *If any of your benefits are taxable for 2013 **and** they include a lump-sum benefit payment that was for an earlier year, you may be able to reduce the taxable amount. See Pub. 915 for details.*

or its employees or officers are qualified to provide tax advice.

53

You can reduce the income taxes that you are paying on your Social Security Income.

Using the worksheet on the previous page as an example, 50% of the Social Security Income was taxable. However, if income on line 4 and municipal bond interest on line 5 were $78,000 combined instead of $34,800, as much as 85% of the Social Security income can be taxable. Yes 85%!

However, you can now have more income as a result of less taxes on Social Security income if you reposition some of your money in the bank (line 3) and in Municipal Bonds (line 4) into a tax-deferred annuity and not withdraw the interest.

How much more income can you get? Simply multiply your tax bracket times the amount reported on line 18. So if you are in a 28% tax bracket, you can have $1,232 more in spendable income since 28% times $4,400, the number reported on line 18 of the worksheet on the previous page, is $1,232.

And, you can buy or do a lot of neat things with $1,232 like:
- See 52 movies a year.
- Laugh and have fun at a nearby resort every quarter.
- Get the best seat at Yankee Stadium every other year.

Note:
Since the officers, directors and employees of W.V.H., Inc. are not qualified to provide tax advice, we have this worksheet without any added numbers on page 349 so you can take it to your tax advisor for completion. After completion, consider reaching out to your insurance and/or investment professional.

Next Steps
- Consult with your tax and legal advisors.
- Based upon their recommendation, reach out to your insurance professional and/or investment professional.
- Action begins with a decision.
- Take cautious baby steps.
- Diversify.

Your annuity can be protected from creditors if you live in the right states.

An annuity should not be purchased solely because your state can protect your annuity dollars from creditors. Your state could change how they protect annuity owners and annuitants from creditors, you could move to another state, or your creditor's attorney could successfully find a loophole. However, if you live in the "right state," it is a nice extra benefit to have. Interested? Turn the page to find out how your money can potentially be protected from creditors if you live in the right state.

Your annuity can be protected from creditors if you live in the right states.

W hile we are not qualified to discuss this topic of creditor protection, we do feel comfortable strongly recommending that you consult an attorney who specializes in this field in your state. Said differently, states vary widely on how they treat creditors relating to divorce, child support, and the number of months between the annuity purchase and creditor claim. And, naturally, states cannot stop the IRS from getting at your money.

In general, some states can protect annuity dollars in 2 broad categories. Category 1: Dollars in non-qualified annuities, in other words, money that you have earned, paid taxes on, and put into an annuity instead of a taxable account like a CD. Category 2: Dollars in some qualified retirement accounts like IRAs.

Category 1: Money In Non-Qualified Annuities

A handful of states protect 100% of the money in the annuity for the annuity owner; a handful of states protect 100% of the money in the annuity for the annuity beneficiary, but not for the owner; a few states protect a dollar amount like $100,000 instead of 100%; some states only protect monthly payments ranging from $300 to $2,000 a month, but mostly in lower range of $300 a month. The balance of the states have no protection at all.

Category 2: Money in Some Qualified Accounts

Over 60% of the states protect 100% of the money in qualified plans; a handful of states only protect dollars necessary to support debtor's living expenses; a handful of states protect a dollar limit such as $50,000-$500,000; a handful of states have no protection at all.

Turn the page to examine your Next Steps.

The Number Of States That Protect Annuity Dollars in Annuity Contracts From Creditors

YES	NO
0	States	50

100% of the money in an annuity is protected for the annuity owner

YES	NO
0	States	50

100% of the money in an annuity is protected for the annuity beneficiary; not the owner

YES	NO
0	States	50

Up to $100,000 for annuity owner or beneficiary

YES	NO
0	States	50

Monthly payment from $300 to $2,000 is protected for the annuitant

Summary: 50% of the states have some protection while 50% have no protection

The Number Of States That Protect Some Qualified Money Such As IRAs From Creditors

YES	NO
0	States	50

100% of the money in most types of qualified plans are protected

YES	NO
0	States	50

Dollars necessary for support of debtor and family are protected

YES	NO
0	States	50

Amounts ranging from $50,000 to $500,000 in most types of qualified plans are protected

Summary: More than 40 states have some sort of protection for dollars in most qualified plans such as IRAs. Less than 10 states have no protection at all.

All parties should consult their legal advisors about the above, how federal bankruptcy protects some qualified retirement plans, and how withdrawals from the above accounts might be accessible to creditors.

Your annuity can be protected from creditors if you live in the right states.

Next Steps

- Consult with your tax and legal advisors regarding creditor protection and for the names of local attorneys who specialize in this field; then contact the specialist attorney.

- Rather than rely on creditor protection from your state, examine ways to insure yourself from potential problems by getting special insurance that covers malpractice, errors and omissions, copyright infringement, communications liability, internet cyberspace, and workman's compensation by reaching out to insurance professionals who specialize in those lines.

- Reach out to your insurance professional regarding products that can potentially insulate your dollars from creditors.

- Circle back to your tax and legal advisors regarding the products that you are considering.

- Take cautious baby steps.

- Diversify.

- Read what you are about to sign.

A non-qualified annuity's tax advantages are overlooked by most IRA owners.

As you are aware, the government has extended tax advantages to qualified retirement plans such as 401(k)s and IRAs where you can get tax-deferred accumulation with a wide variety of investments including Certificates of Deposit and Mutual Funds. What you may not be aware of is that the government has also extended tax advantages to non-qualified annuities: Fixed and Variable. Turn the page if you want to discover special tax advantages that most IRA owners overlook.

55

A non-qualified annuity's tax advantages are overlooked by most IRA owners.

Y ou could say that a non-qualified annuity picks up from where your existing IRA leaves off because just like your IRA, earnings accumulate without current taxes, income taxes are paid when interest is withdrawn, and, there is a 10% excise tax penalty if dollars are withdrawn prior to age 59.5.

However, unlike your IRA, there is no maximum on how much money you can put into your non-qualified annuity since the premium is not tax deductible. Plus you don't have to begin taking dollars out at the age of 70.5.

Do you agree with others when they say that "The non-qualified annuity picks up from where your IRA leaves off?"

A Non-Qualified Annuity Can Pick Up Where Your IRA Leaves Off

JUST LIKE YOUR IRA:

- Interest accumulates free of current taxes.

- Withdrawals are taxable.

- Excise tax penalties exist.

UNLIKE YOUR IRA:

- Not tax deductible.

- No maximum premium*.

- No maximum age*.

- Can defer distributions after age 70.5.

*Imposed by tax law

All parties should see the insurer disclosure and annuity contract for guaranteed interest rates and values. Bank CDs are insured up to applicable limits by the FDIC. Annuities are NOT insured by the FDIC or any other agency and are subject to investment risks, including the possible loss of principal. The guarantees in an annuity contract are subject to the claims-paying ability of the insurer making the guarantees. Annuities have earnings which are taxable upon withdrawal and, if taken before age 59.5, may be subject to a 10% Federal early withdrawal penalty. Annuities can have a surrender charge period of 10 years or more.

A non-qualified annuity's tax advantages are overlooked by most IRA owners.

Next Steps

- Consult with your tax and legal advisors.
- Based upon the recommendation of your advisor, reach out to your insurance professional and/or investment professional.
- Action begins with a decision.
- Take cautious baby steps.
- Diversify.

secret **56**

Almost all annuity presentations could be as simple as this one.

People buy simple things, things they understand. The annuity presentation that best describes the benefits to transferring some of your money at the bank into an annuity is on the following page. Would you like to read a real simple explanation? If so, please turn the page now.

Almost all annuity presentations could be as simple as this one.

Another way you can illustrate the power of tax deferral is to show this comparison on the opposite page. We refer to it as "KIS" because we Keep It Simple.

Once again, we are comparing a Fixed Annuity with a long-term interest rate guarantee to a Certificate of Deposit. Notice the simplicity:

The Amount of Principal/Premium is $100,000. Interest rates are 4% for each. Interest earned is $4,000 with each.

Where does the interest go? Under your taxable alternative, $2,880 stays with you each and every year. The balance, $1,120, goes to the government in taxes (assuming a 28% tax bracket). On the annuity side, the entire $4,000 can stay with you to compound more interest.

How can your money grow? In ten short years, you can have $132,834 if you stay where you are and $148,024 if you simply reposition your money to an annuity.

Would you like a simple and secure way to potentially accumulate more money? Unquestionably, when you combine the above words with the important disclosure beneath the chart on the next page with the advice from your tax and legal advisors, you are one step closer to owning an annuity you understand.

Taxable vs. Tax-Deferred

	Taxable Alternative	Tax-Deferred Annuity
Interest	4%	4%
Amount of interest earned	$4,000	$4,000
Where does the interest go?	You keep $2,880 You pay $1,120	You keep $4,000
How can money grow?	10 years $132,834	10 years $148,024
	20 years $176,449	20 years $219,112

The interest rates for the Tax-Deferred Fixed Annuity are hypothetical since interest rates vary by product and carrier. All parties should see the insurer disclosure and annuity contract for guaranteed interest rates and values. This hypothetical example assumes a $100,000 premium, a 4% interest rate, a 28% tax bracket, and is for illustrative purposes only. Bank CDs are insured up to applicable limits by the FDIC. Annuities are insurance products and are NOT insured by the FDIC or any other federal government agency. The guarantees in an annuity contract are subject to the claims paying ability of the insurer making the guarantees. Annuities have earnings which are taxable upon withdrawal and if taken before age 59.5, may be subject to IRS penalties. Withdrawals taken during the Surrender Charge period above the penalty-free amount will be subject to Surrender Charges and a possible Market Value Adjustment.

Almost all annuity presentations could be as simple as this one.

Next Steps

- Consult with your tax and legal advisors.

- Based upon the recommendation of your advisors, reach out to your insurance professional and/or investment professional.

- Action begins with a decision.

- Take cautious baby steps.

- Diversify.

You can now get tax deferral and monthly income at the same time.

Imagine putting $100,000 into 2 annuities and receiving a check of $263.00 a month for ten years in which 92% of it is income tax free; and still have $100,000 remaining in your tax-deferred annuity at the end of ten years. Would you be interested? Would you be more interested if it were guaranteed? The next page shows you how it can be done by using 2 different annuities.

57
You can now get tax deferral and monthly income at the same time.

In the example on the opposite page, we select two different types of annuities. Independently, each type has its own advantages, but when they are combined, they become a powerful way to receive tax-advantaged income and tax-deferred accumulation at the same time.

Before we explain how it is done and the possible disadvantages, let's "hear" how an insurance professional might accurately explain it.

"You can put $100,000 into 2 annuities, receive a check of $263 a month for ten years in which 92% of it is income tax-free, and still have $100,000 remaining in your tax-deferred annuity at the end of ten years."

How is it done? Very simply! Please look at the opposite page. The annuity in the right column is a Fixed Annuity with a ten year interest rate guarantee of 3.5%. The annuity in the left column is an Immediate Annuity: 10 Year Period Certain.

The hypothetical Fixed Annuity in the right column has a ten year interest rate guarantee, hence, a guaranteed accumulation value every year. Said differently, the $70,892 placed into the Fixed Annuity is guaranteed to be $100,000 in 10 years since it is guaranteed in the annuity contract by the insurance company crediting 3.5% interest.

The hypothetical Immediate Annuity in the left column gives you a guaranteed monthly check of $263* every month for 10 years. At the end of 10 years, monthly payments stop since the Immediate Annuity chosen was for a Period Certain of 10 Years (but Period Certains guaranteeing lower payments of up to 30 years are available too).

*Hypothetical
(Continued on page 230)

Original Premium
$100,000

Split this way
via 2 separate applications

$29,108	$70,892
Immediate Annuity	**Tax-Deferred Annuity**
Amount to provide Tax-Favored income	Amount to grow Tax-Deferred
$263	$100,000
Guaranteed monthly income for 10 years	Value in 10 years using an interest rate of 3.5% for 10 years
92%	
% of annuity payment which may be excludable from taxes	

The interest rates for the Tax-Deferred Fixed Annuity are hypothetical since interest rates vary by product and carrier. All parties should see the insurer disclosure and annuity contract for guaranteed interest rates and values. This hypothetical example assumes a $100,000 premium, a 3.5% interest rate, a 28% tax bracket, and is for illustrative purposes only. Bank CDs are insured up to applicable limits by the FDIC. Annuities are insurance products and are NOT insured by the FDIC or any other federal government agency. The guarantees in an annuity contract are subject to the claims-paying ability of the insurer making the guarantees. Annuities have earnings which are taxable upon withdrawal and, if taken before age 59.5, may be subject to IRS penalties. Withdrawals taken during the Surrender Charge period above the penalty-free amount will be subject to Surrender Charges and a possible Market Value Adjustment.

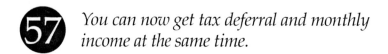

57

You can now get tax deferral and monthly income at the same time.

(Continued from page 228)

At the end of ten years, the annuity owner can 1) surrender the Fixed Annuity and pay income taxes on the tax-deferred interest of $29,108, 2) do a tax-free exchange by exchanging the Fixed Annuity to another Fixed Annuity, or 3) renew the Fixed Annuity with the same insurer for another period of years.

If income is still desired, the annuity owner can a) "annuitize" the entire Fixed Annuity and receive a higher monthly payout, or b) receive income from the Fixed Annuity via fully taxable withdrawals.

2013 Update: Possible New Alternative For Year 11
With your tax advisor's OK, consider re-splitting your $100,000 again. Just reposition conceptually $29,108 that is in your $100,000 tax-deferred annuity into a Period Certain Immediate Annuity. (with annual payments beginning at end of year one) via a Partial 1035 Exchange. In the opinion of some, the IRS release of Revenue Procedure 2011-38 addresses important issues for Partial 1035 exchanges after Oct. 24th, 2011.

1. The new rules expressly allow partial 1035 exchanges from tax-deferred annuities to immediate annuities, however, payouts from the immediate annuity must begin no earlier than 180 days. Hence, the reason the new Period Certain annuity should make payments annually, at least, for year one.

2. The immediate annuity must either have a life contingency like 10 Year Certain and Life or a Period Certain longer than 10 years.

Note: The exclusion ratio during the second "split" might be around 65% since 29.1% of the $29,108 was tax-deferred interest from the tax-deferred annuity.

Next Steps

- Consult with your tax and legal advisors.

- Reach out to your insurance professional regarding products that can give you both tax-deferred accumulation and income.

- Circle back to your tax and legal advisors regarding the products that you are considering to buy.

secret

You can exchange an annuity for another annuity income tax free if you do it the IRS way.

Annuities are awarded with so many tax advantages such as 1) tax deferral, 2) the spousal beneficiary being able to continue tax deferral indefinitely, 3) a tax-free exclusion on some income received, and 4) the unique opportunity to do a 1035 tax-free exchange to another annuity if you do it the IRS way. Turn the page to learn how to get a better annuity for your annuity dollars.

58

You can exchange an annuity for another annuity income tax free if you do it the IRS way.

The Internal Revenue Service calls it a 1035(a) tax-free exchange. We call it a blessing. Simply put, if you follow the advice of your tax advisor, you can exchange your non-qualified* annuity for another annuity income tax free.

The 1035 exchange is a unique opportunity, but remember to be careful.

What advice will your tax advisor give you? Since they are more qualified in tax matters** than we, they might say that you should:

1. If you are exchanging a non-qualified annuity, assign the old annuity contract to the new insurer; in other words, the check goes directly from the old insurer to the new insurer .

2. Keep the owner, annuitant, and beneficiary designations in the new annuity the same as in the old annuity contract.

3. Make sure that the exchange is "like for like," for example, exchanging an annuity for a life insurance policy is not a "like for like" exchange and your tax advisor can offer other examples.

4. Be careful if you are considering exchanging only some of the money inside of your annuity. This is called a Partial Exchange that has its own set of conditions.

Bottom line: This 1035(a) exchange is a unique opportunity but be careful. Also, find out, before the exchange, if there are any surrender charges and/or a market value adjustment for leaving the old annuity and if you will lose any tax advantages or other benefits by leaving the old annuity. Said differently, you want to gain by the exchange almost immediately instead of having to wait years and years before the exchange benefits.

*Your non-qualified annuity is one that has your after-tax personal savings, not the annuity where you have your IRA, 401(k), 403(b) money since those are called qualified annuities.(Discussed in Secret 52)

**The copyright owner of this book, W.V.H., Inc., and its employees, officers, and directors are NOT qualified or trained to provide tax or legal advice and all parties are urged to consult with their own tax, legal, and financial advisors.

Steps To Follow For Exchanging An Annuity Income Tax Free

1. Assign*

2. Same designations

3. Like for like

4. Consult with your tax advisors

*Assumes total exchange of Non-Qualified Annuity: Consult with your tax advisors regarding partial and total exchanges.

What is best for you depends upon your circumstances. Turn the page to learn what your next steps could be. This secret is not investment advice, but it is a suggestion that you should think about your retirement savings regularly.

You can exchange an annuity for another annuity income tax free if you do it the IRS way.

Next Steps

- Consult with your tax and legal advisors.

- Reach out to your insurance professional regarding products that can accumulate more money for you.

- Ask your insurance and/or investment professional if there are any surrender charges and/or a market value adjustment if you exchange the old annuity for a new annuity.

- Take cautious baby steps.

- Circle back to your tax and legal advisors regarding the products that you are considering.

- Understand and read what you are about to sign.

secret **59**

An annuity is more apt to provide liquidity when you need it; a CD when you don't need it.

W hile you should probably own both Certificates of Deposit and Tax-Deferred Annuities, we must recognize that each one offers different benefits, and liquidity is one of the distinguishing elements. Ironically, some people choose CDs over annuities since they think that CDs are more liquid than annuities. If you turn the page, you will discover that an annuity can offer you more liquidity than a CD at a time when you are more apt to need it.

59

An annuity is more apt to provide liquidity when you need it; a CD when you don't need it.

F

ortunately, there is only a slight difference as to how Certificates of Deposit and Tax-Deferred Annuities offer you partial access to your money. Most Certificates of Deposit give you penalty-free access to your interest during the interest rate guarantee period. On the other hand, most annuities offer you insurance company penalty-free access to 10% of your annuity account.* One could say that there is a small difference between the two as it pertains to partial access especially for annuity owners 59.5 and older (the age in which the 10% tax penalty disappears).

However, there is a major difference to getting penalty-free access to "all of your money," but allow us to ask you one question before we explain. When are you more apt to need a lot of your money? In the next 5 years? Or is your emergency more apt to occur sometime after the next 5 years? Let's ask it a different way. When is a nursing home confinement or some major emergency more apt to occur? In the next 5 years or later in life, if ever?

As you will soon see, too many are selecting a Certificate of Deposit to provide liquidity at the wrong time. With Certificates of Deposit, you get penalty-free access to 100% of your money at the end of each guarantee period, but you will have to pay loss of interest penalties if you ever need your principal during the guarantee interest period. So with a one year or five year CD, you only have penalty-free access to 100% of your principal at the end of the term such as at the end of one year for a one year CD and at the end of five years for a five year CD.

As you see in the chart on the opposite page, in the next 25 years (9,125 days), there will be only five times in which you will be able to gain penalty-free access to 100 % of your money if you have a five year CD. What are the chances of your emergency occurring during those magical 5 times? Slim or none?

There can be a federal tax penalty of 10% for withdrawals prior to age 59.5.

Liquidity Comparison Between A CD And An Annuity

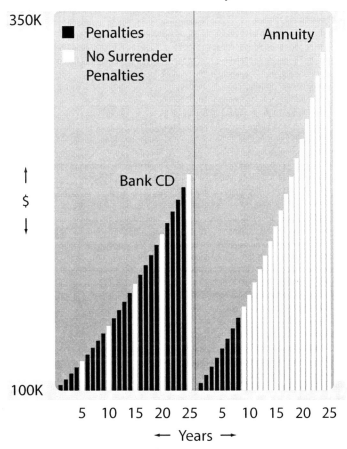

The interest rates for the Tax-Deferred Fixed Annuity and 5-year CD are hypothetical since interest rates vary by product, carrier, and bank. All parties should see the insurer disclosure and annuity contract for guaranteed interest rates and values. This hypothetical example assumes a $100,000 premium, a 5% interest rate, a 28% tax bracket, an 8-year surrender charge period with a surrender charge of 8% in year one decreasing 1% each year to 0% in year 9 with no market value adjustment, and is for illustrative purposes only. Bank CDs are insured up to applicable limits by the FDIC. Annuities are insurance products and are NOT insured by the FDIC or any other federal government agency. The guarantees in an annuity contract are subject to the claims-paying ability of the insurer making the guarantees. Annuities have earnings which are taxable upon withdrawal and, if taken before age 59.5, may be subject to IRS penalties. Withdrawals taken during the Surrender Charge period above the penalty-free amount will be subject to Surrender Charges and a possible Market Value Adjustment.

An annuity is more apt to provide liquidity when you need it; a CD when you don't need it.

With many annuities, the insurance company penalties exist only during the initial five year, seven year, or ten year plus surrender charge period. In other words, the surrender charges can disappear to zero after the surrender charge period. Therefore, as you will see in the chart on the previous page, in the next 25 years (again, 9,125 days), there will be 6,205 days in which you can have insurance company penalty-free access to all of your money assuming a surrender charge period of 8 years. With the bank 5 year CD, there are only 50 days in which you can have penalty-free access to your principal, assuming the bank gives you a 10 day grace period at the end of each CD maturity to withdraw your deposit. Is your emergency more apt to occur in the 6,205 annuity days or in the 50 bank days?

This does *not* mean that annuities should be chosen to fulfill short-term liquidity needs too. No! At the least, you should have six months' income in 30, 90, 180 day, and 1 year certificates of deposit. Annuities and the tax advantages awarded to them are designed to help people accumulate more money for retirement, hence, the reason there is a 10% excise tax penalty for withdrawals or surrenders before age 59.5.

To summarize, when your emergency arises, consider turning to your Money Market account first. Need more money, go to your passbook savings. Need more money, go to your short-term 30-90 day CDs. Need more money, go to your longer term CDs like one to five years and withdraw interest first and consider withdrawing the principal. Need more money, turn to your insurer penalty free 10% withdrawal from your annuity.

Next Steps

- Consult with your tax and legal advisors.

- Reach out to your insurance professional for annuities with reasonable surrender charges.

- Take cautious baby steps.

- Circle back to your tax and legal advisors regarding the products that you are considering.

- Understand and read what you are about to sign.

60

There are 7 ways to receive guaranteed monthly income.

Insurance companies are the only "franchise" that can guarantee lifetime income even if you live to 120 and longer. Historically, "annuitization" has been the most popular and common way to receive guaranteed income from your annuity. Just recently, a rider has been added to many annuities that has many of the benefits of "annuitization" but without some of the disadvantages. But, since all choices have both advantages and disadvantages, let's turn the page to learn about each way to receiving guaranteed income.

60 *There are 7 ways to receive guaranteed monthly income.*

W e all want financial and emotional independence but few of us have it since we fear outliving our money and what happens afterwards. One solution would be turning to an insurance company; more specifically, to an immediate annuity where income could begin immediately. Others, knowing that they would need guaranteed income later, not now, have been purchasing Tax-Deferred Annuities that guaranteed them the right to guaranteed income later instead of now. And, just recently, Lifetime Income Riders have been added to some annuities that offer a new interesting way to receive guaranteed income.

On the opposite page, we show how much monthly income can be guaranteed for an individual age 65 with a premium of $100,000 based on the some of the settlement options. Below and on page 242 we give you a description of each settlement option. Remember, all products and concepts have advantages and disadvantages. You just need to know them so you stay informed.

Period Certain
Level payments are made for a fixed number of years. If the annuitant dies before the period expires, the payments will continue to the named beneficiary until the expiration of the certain period. Usually the minimum period is 5 years and the maximum is 30 years.

Life Only
Life Only provides level payments during the lifetime of the annuitant. At the time of the annuitant's death, the payments stop without refund or continuation regardless of how many payments have been made.

Life With Period Certain
Life annuity with a period certain provides level payments during the lifetime of the annuitant. If the annuitant dies before the period certain expires, for example 10 years, the payments will continue to the named beneficiary until the expiration of the certain period.

(Continued on page 242)

There Are 7 Ways To Receive Guaranteed Monthly Income

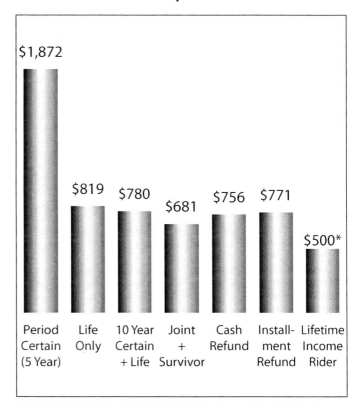

*Access to contract value is available
Assuming a premium of $100,000 and a couple age 65

What is best for you depends upon your circumstances. Turn the page to learn what your next steps could be. This secret is not investment advice, but it is a suggestion that you should think about your retirement savings regularly.

There are 7 ways to receive guaranteed monthly income.

(Continued from page 240)

Joint and Survivor

The Joint and Survivor annuity provides payments during the lifetimes of two annuitants and stops at the death of the last remaining survivor. Again, the owner may add a guarantee period certain of 10 years to 30 years. Payments usually remain level but variations like Joint and Survivor 2/3 and Joint and Survivor 50% are available. Simply put, payments to the survivor would decrease a third or a half depending upon the option selected.

Cash Refund

Level payments are made during the lifetime of the annuitant. When the annuitant dies, if sum total of all payments received is less than the dollars annuitized, the balance is paid to the beneficiary.

Installment Refunds

Payments are made to the annuitant. When the annuitant dies, if the sum of all payments made is less than the dollars annuitized, payments will continue to the named beneficiary until the payments to annuitant and beneficiary equal the dollars annuitized.

Lifetime Income Rider

While Secret 65 and 68 explain this unique rider in more detail, the Lifetime Income Rider can guarantee lifetime income, for example, 5% of the Income Benefit Base. And, unlike, all of the above options, you can ask payments to stop and surrender your annuity and potentially gain access to your annuity dollars.

Next Steps

- Consult with your tax, legal, and financial advisors.
- Reach out to your insurance professional regarding products that can give you lifetime income.
- Circle back to your tax and legal advisors regarding the products that you are considering.
- Diversify.
- Understand and read what you are about to sign.

61

The worst case annuity scenario is a nice worst case scenario to have.

I t is often helpful to look at the almost worst case scenario before selecting a financial product. And, since an annuity is a long-term vehicle designed for a long term need, Retirement, let's look at what happens if you buy an annuity and surrender it almost right away. When you turn the page, you will discover that while surrendering an annuity during the surrender charge period is not a wise thing to do, there are a lot of other financial alternatives out there with a far greater penalty.

61

The worst case annuity scenario is a nice worst case scenario to have.

It is interesting to show what happens when an annuity owner surrenders their money before the surrender charge period ends. Admittedly, there will be a cost, but it's this modest cost with some annuities that can help you to appreciate how low the penalties can be.

The chart on the opposite page assumes a $100,000 premium in a hypothetical annuity crediting 5% interest, but this concept works at any interest rate. The surrender charges assumed are 8% in year 1 declining 1% each year to 0% in year 9. Look what happens when one surrenders and surrender charges are deducted from the annuity value. Even if you surrender at the end of year 1 and after surrender charges are deducted, you still would have $96,600.00. Do you know of any other products that can have a minus 3.4% return in an almost worst case scenario, a surrender in year 1? Look at the return if you surrender at the end of year 2 (a positive 2.5% over 2 years), year 3 (a positive 8.8% over 3 years), and year 4 (a positive 15.5% over 4 years).

Are we saying that an annuity is a one year commitment? No, we are saying that the annuity penalties can be minor compared to other financial alternatives like buying a stock or mutual fund right before the beginning of a Bear Market or buying a gorgeous home right before the next housing crisis. Too many times, consumers who hear about a surrender charge period think that they cannot surrender their money until the penalty period is over. This idea shows that you can get access to your money at a price few other financial retirement products could match. Can the penalties be greater than shown on the opposite page? Absolutely, if you were to buy an annuity policy where the surrender charges were greater than 8% in the first year or if the surrender charge period were greater than eight years, or if the annuity had a negative Market Value Adjustment, then the penalties would be greater.

The Gain Or (Loss) When You Surrender Each Year

Year	Hypothetical Fixed Annuity Value at 5%	Surrender Charge	Cash Surrender Value	Gain (Loss)
1	$105,000	8%	$96,600	(-3.4%)
2	$110,250	7%	$102,532	2.5%
3	$115,763	6%	$108,817	8.8%
4	$121,551	5%	$115,474	15.5%
5	$127,628	4%	$122,523	22.5%
6	$134,010	3%	$129,990	30.0%
7	$140,710	2%	$137,896	37.9%
8	$147,746	1%	$146,269	46.3%
9	$155,132	0%	$155,132	55.0%

The fifth column in the above chart calculates the percentage change in the initial premium based on a total surrender each year. For example, if they surrendered at the end of the first year, an 8% surrender charge imposed on the total hypothetical value would have resulted in a Cash Surrender Value of $96,600, a 3.4% decrease on the initial $100,000 premium. If the annuity contract waived surrender charges for a partial 10% withdrawal preceding a surrender, the above percentage decrease would be less and increases would be even greater for the annuity owner.

The above chart assumes a $100,000 premium, a hypothetical annuity crediting an interest rate of 5% each year, an 8-year surrender charge period with a surrender charge of 8% in year one decreasing 1% each year to 0% in year 9 with no market value adjustment. In actuality, interest rates vary by product and carrier and all parties should see the insurer disclosure and annuity contract for guaranteed interest rates, values, surrender charges, and a market value adjustment, if any. Guarantees are subject to the claims-paying ability of the particular insurer.

The worst case annuity scenario is a nice worst case scenario to have.

Next Steps

- Consult with your tax and legal advisors.

- Reach out to your insurance and/or investment professional for products that have a reasonable surrender charge period.

- Diversify.

- Keep at least 6 months' income in highly liquid FDIC accounts.

- Circle back to your tax and legal advisors regarding the products that you are considering.

> Bank CDs are insured up to applicable limits by the FDIC. Annuities are insurance products and are NOT insured by the FDIC or any other federal government agency. The guarantees in an annuity contract are subject to the claims-paying ability of the insurer making the guarantees. Annuities have earnings which are taxable upon withdrawal and, if taken before age 59.5, may be subject to IRS penalties. Withdrawals taken during the surrender charge period above the penalty-free amount will be subject to Surrender Charges and a possible Market Value Adjustment.

Who you designate as annuitant and beneficiary can be a costly mistake.

W hile most of the secrets in this book help you accumulate more money, this is the only secret that can help prevent you from losing ALL of your money. Before we start, do not become alarmed since you can easily and quickly fix a potential mistake that you may have made when completing your annuity application as long as you fix the mistake before the annuity owner and/or annuitant dies. Are you concerned? If so, please turn the page.

62

Who you designate as annuitant and beneficiary can be a costly mistake.

Too many annuity owners or spouses have "lost their annuity money" while they were still alive. Now that we have your attention, allow us to explain so you can easily fix this problem before it is too late.

For example, last year, Baskin bought a $300,000 Tax-Deferred Annuity. On the application, he named himself as the owner, his wife, Robin, as annuitant, and their only son, Heath, as the beneficiary.

Sadly, Baskin died. The insurance company promptly paid the $300,000 plus all interest to the son, the one named as beneficiary on the annuity application. In other words, the wife, Robin, saw "her $300,000" disappear in spite of the will designating Robin as the sole heir to Baskin's assets.

Explanation Of Problem

Every annuity application and annuity contract has 3 very important designations: owner, annuitant, and beneficiary.

The *owner* decides when to withdraw, surrender or annuitize, names the annuitant and beneficiaries on the annuity application, and can make changes later.

The *annuitant*—often the same person as the owner—is the one who receives lifetime income from the insurer if the owner ever annuitizes.

The *beneficiary* is the one who gets the death benefit—often the entire annuity value—when either the owner or annuitant dies.

THIS BECOMES THE PROBLEM. IF THE OWNER AND THE ANNUITANT ARE DIFFERENT PEOPLE, SOME ANNUITY CONTRACTS PAY A DEATH BENEFIT IF THE OWNER DIES AND SOME ANNUITY CONTRACTS PAY A DEATH BENEFIT IF THE ANNUITANT DIES.

(Continued on page 250)

The Big Difference Between Owner and Annuitant Driven Contracts

Owner* Driven Annuity Contract				
Owner	Annuitant	Beneficiary	Who Dies	Who Gets the Death Benefit
Baskin	Robin[1]	Heath	Baskin	Heath
Baskin	Robin	Robin	Baskin	Robin
Baskin & Robin as joint owners	Robin	Primary: Baskin & Robin Contingent: Heath	Baskin	Robin
Annuitant* Driven Annuity Contract				
Baskin	Robin	Heath	Baskin	Nobody (owner died)
Baskin	Robin	Baskin	Robin	Baskin
Baskin & Robin as joint owners	Baskin & Robin as joint annuitants[2]	Primary: Baskin & Robin Contingent: Heath	Baskin	Robin[3]

*What triggers death benefit
1 Spouse
2 Non-spouse
3 With many annuity contracts, spousal beneficiary may continue annuity indefinitely

What is best for you depends upon your circumstances. Turn the page to learn what your next steps could be. This secret is not investment advice, but it is a suggestion that you should think about your retirement savings regularly.

All parties should see the insurer disclosure and annuity contract for guaranteed interest rates and values. Bank CDs are insured up to applicable limits by the FDIC. Annuities are insurance products and are NOT insured by the FDIC or any other federal government agency. The guarantees in an annuity contract are subject to the claims-paying ability of the insurer making the guarantees. Annuities have earnings which are taxable upon withdrawal and, if taken before age 59.5, may be subject to IRS penalties. Withdrawals taken during the Surrender Charge period above the penalty-free amount will be subject to Surrender Charges and a possible Market Value Adjustment.

62 *Who you designate as annuitant and beneficiary can be a costly mistake.*

(Continued from page 248)

On the opposite page, we show potential problems and potential solutions for your tax and legal advisors to review since we are not qualified to offer tax, legal or investment advice. Want to correct the problem? Read the Next Steps at the bottom of the page.

3 things to consider

1. Not all annuity contracts are the same as it relates to when a death benefit is paid. Some annuity contracts pay a death benefit to a beneficiary when the owner dies while other annuity contracts pay a death benefit to the beneficiary when the annuitant dies. Fortunately, it is clearly spelled out in your annuity contract.

2. The party the owner designates as the beneficiary on an application for an annuity is legally binding in spite of the will saying something to the contrary.

3. Try to have the owner and annuitant as the same person.

Next Steps

- Consult with your tax and legal advisors.

- Contact the insurance company and find out right away who the owner, the annuitant, and beneficiaries are for your annuity.

- Find out if your annuity is "owner-driven" meaning the death benefit is paid out if the owner dies or if your annuity contract is "annuitant-driven" meaning the death benefit is paid out if the annuitant dies.

- Consult with your tax and legal advisors.

- If a change is required like a beneficiary change, reach out to your insurance or investment professional, complete the Insurance Company Change Request Form, make a copy, and mail it return receipt requested to the insurer.

- Await confirmation from the insurer that the change has been made.

secret (63)

A 412(e)3 Pension Plan is the most overlooked buying opportunity by small business owners

If more "seasoned" small business owners knew that there was a pension plan that allowed them to set aside unusually large contributions, deduct 100% of the contributions, and watch their contributions accumulate tax deferred, then the 412(e)3 Pension Plan would not be one of the biggest secrets in the financial services industry. If you are age 50 and older and own a small business, turn the page for maybe the quickest way to accumulate one million dollars.

63

A 412(e)3 Pension Plan is the most overlooked buying opportunity by small business owners.

A 412(e)3 is a tax qualified Defined Benefit Pension Plan ideal for some small business owners who are age 50 or older, have younger employees, have no more than 5 employees, have large profits each year, and pay a lot of income taxes. As you will soon see, the 412(e)3 can reduce the owner's income taxes appreciably.

On the opposite page, we show a hypothetical small business where the owner, Peter, is 57, his wife, Mary, is age 55 and his computer programmer, Paul, is age 45 when the 412(e)3 plan was started. Please notice that contributions for Peter alone were between $73,000 and $94,000 during the first 6 years. In fact, after 6 short years, Peter would have accumulated over $568,000. Combined with his wife, Mary, they would have accumulated almost $700,000. At age 65, they would have well over one million dollars. Do you know of a faster way to accumulate $1,000,000?

However, that is only part of the story. Since 412(e)3s must be funded by Fixed Annuities or by Fixed Annuities and life insurance combined, the assets are guaranteed by the claims paying ability of the insurance company issuing the annuity. In other words, the smaller contributions and the potential risk you get with 401(k) or other Defined Contribution plans are replaced with LARGE tax-deductible contributions and guaranteed growth such as 3.5% interest.

Are there other advantages? Yes, you can have a 3 year vesting so employees who leave you prematurely cannot take your contribution with them and plan administration can be simpler than many other types of pension plans. Are there any disadvantages? Sure, there are disadvantages with every financial product. However, your circumstances will allow your tax and legal advisor and insurance professional to verbalize what you need to know.

How A 412(e)3 Pension Plan Can Accumulate So Much Money So Quickly

Name	Age	Salary	Annual Contributions (Contribution for years, 2, 4 & 5 are not shown.)			Accumulated Value
			Year 1	Year 3	Year 6	End of Year 6
Peter	57	$172,245	$73,064	$85,239	$94,056	$568,260
Paul	45	$68,910	$25,432	$42,687	$32,584	$227,015
Mary	55	$33,856	$16,014	$10,569	$17,838	$100,140

The above chart shows a hypothetical 412(e)3 pension plan for a corporation with three employees.

What is best for you depends upon your circumstances. Turn the page to learn what your next steps could be. This secret is not investment advice, but it is a suggestion that you should think about your retirement savings regularly.

All parties should see the insurer disclosure and annuity contract for guaranteed interest rates and values. Bank CDs are insured up to applicable limits by the FDIC. Annuities are insurance products and are NOT insured by the FDIC or any other federal government agency. The guarantees in an annuity contract are subject to the claims-paying ability of the insurer making the guarantees. Annuities have earnings which are taxable upon withdrawal and, if taken before age 59.5, may be subject to IRS penalties. Withdrawals taken during the Surrender Charge period above the penalty-free amount will be subject to Surrender Charges and a possible Market Value Adjustment.

A 412(e)3 Pension Plan is the most overlooked buying opportunity by small business owners.

Next Steps

- Consult with your tax and legal advisors.
- Reach out to your insurance professional regarding 412(e)3 pension plans.
- Take cautious baby steps.
- Circle back to your tax and legal advisors regarding the 412(e)3 and insurer that you are considering.
- Diversify.
- Understand and read what you are about to sign.
- If the annuity used for the 412(e)3 is an unallocated annuity, ask your state department of insurance if their Guaranty Association covers or excludes unallocated annuity contracts.

Some annuities can give you a guaranteed selling price for every year.

Fixed and Variable Annuities offer different advantages. One advantage with many Fixed Annuities is that you can receive a guaranteed selling price since the surrender charges and interest rate guarantees are expressed in the annuity contract. Wouldn't it be great if you could purchase a home or stock or bond and be guaranteed the selling price for any time in the future? Now, turn the page to see examples of other products that have and do not have a guaranteed selling price.

64 *Some annuities can give you a guaranteed selling price for every year.*

Let's assume that you were able to buy 1,000 shares of stock today in Disney at $50 a share. And, two years from now, you need that money. What would you be able to sell those 1,000 shares of Disney stock for if we were in the middle of a market slump? You don't know, do you?

Let's make believe you put $100,000 in a Municipal Bond. And, two years from now, you need the money. What would you be able to sell that Muni-Bond for if interest rates were then so much higher than when you purchased the Muni-Bond two years earlier? You don't know, do you?

And, what about that gorgeous $500,000 home overlooking the fifth fairway? If you were to buy that home and if you wanted to sell it two years from now, how long would it take you to sell it? And, what would you sell it for?

The surrender charges are the second best thing about owning a Fixed Annuity since the surrender charges are expressed in the annuity contract.

With ninety-nine percent of everything you buy, you have no idea what the selling price is going to be. But, you will know what your selling price is going to be for many Fixed Annuities since the surrender value (selling price) is stated for every year in many Fixed Annuity contracts.

Once and for all, you can get what you want: assurances, guarantees, certainties, and a guaranteed selling price.

Which Products Have A Selling Price?

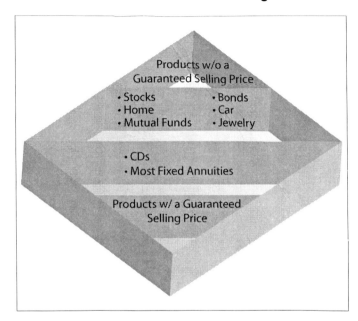

Products w/o a
Guaranteed Selling Price
- Stocks   • Bonds
- Home   • Car
- Mutual Funds • Jewelry

- CDs
- Most Fixed Annuities

Products w/ a Guaranteed
Selling Price

All parties should see the insurer disclosure and annuity contract for guaranteed interest rates and values. Bank CDs are insured up to applicable limits by the FDIC. Annuities are insurance products and are NOT insured by the FDIC or any other federal government agency. The guarantees in an annuity contract are subject to the claims-paying ability of the insurer making the guarantees. Annuities have earnings which are taxable upon withdrawal and, if taken before age 59.5, may be subject to IRS penalties. Withdrawals taken during the Surrender Charge period above the penalty-free amount will be subject to Surrender Charges and a possible Market Value Adjustment.

Some annuities can give you a guaranteed selling price for every year.

Next Steps

- Consult with your tax and legal advisors.

- Reach out to your insurance professional regarding products that can help you accumulate more money. Ask if the recommended annuity has a Market Value Adjustment. If so, ask for the advantages and disadvantages

- Take cautious baby steps.

- Circle back to your tax and legal advisors regarding the products that you are considering.

- Diversify.

- Understand and read what you are about to sign.

You can *now* understand the Guaranteed Minimum Withdrawal Benefit.

T*his secret was written by John Wesley, Director in Product Management at TIAA-CREF; the views expressed in this secret are solely John's views and not necessarily the views of his company.*

How would you like to own a Variable Annuity that guarantees a minimum lifetime withdrawal benefit for you and your spouse while you are invested in the stock market? The income is guaranteed no matter how poorly the stock market performs. You also have the ability to access additional available cash from your annuity account value. At your death, you can leave any remaining balance as an inheritance. Simply turn the page to learn more.

65

You can now understand the Guaranteed Minimum Withdrawal Benefit.

According to LIMRA, an industry research organization, in the second quarter of 2013 the Guaranteed Minimum Lifetime Withdrawal Benefit feature was elected 76% of the time when a Variable Annuity was sold. Does the investor really understand how it works? Let's dig deeper so you can make an informed decision.

This feature was created in 2005 after the stock market decline that began in March 2001 to encourage investors to get back in the stock market. It was a way for insurance companies to differentiate themselves from mutual fund companies. It helped insurers justify the higher costs and suitability issues associated with Variable Annuities. Today, every Variable Annuity contract with a Guaranteed Minimum Lifetime Withdrawal Benefit has different nuances, but the general concept is the same.

The Guaranteed Minimum Lifetime Withdrawal Benefit offers a certain withdrawal amount guaranteed for life. One catch phrase is "5% for life." The fee for this insurance—generally around 1.00% of the income benefit base—must be added to the other expenses associated with the annuity contract. 5% of "what amount?" It might be 5% of your initial investment amount. If you invested $100,000, then the annual guaranteed lifetime withdrawal amount would be $5,000.

Many contracts state that for every year you delay taking the withdrawal, the amount used for the calculation will increase, for example, 5% simple interest. If you delay the payment for 10 years, the income benefit base grows from your initial $100,000 investment to $150,000. Please note that your annuity account value is not guaranteed to grow to $150,000 since market conditions impact gains or losses to your annuity account value.

(Continued on page 262)

Things You Need To Know

3 Reminders

1. If you withdraw your entire account value, your Guaranteed Minimum Lifetime Withdrawal Benefits stop.
2. The guarantee of lifetime income is based upon the financial strength of the insurance companies and their ability to manage this risk. Today, insurance companies limit their exposure to market declines by limiting the asset allocation choices of the investor to a mixture of stocks and bonds.
3. Take money in excess of the withdrawal amount from a different annuity or CD.

4. Each insurance contract has variations on the basic concept of the Guaranteed Minimum Lifetime Withdrawal. Please read the contract carefully.

Checklist

- Do I intend to use the Guaranteed Minimum Lifetime Withdrawal Benefit?
- Do I realize that the percentage of withdrawal does not change once I begin payment?
- Do I realize that the annual guaranteed lifetime withdrawals are first deducted from my own annuity account value?
- Do I know what the additional annual expense for the Guaranteed Minimum Lifetime Withdrawal Benefit is?
- What is the total annual expense for the Variable Annuity with this feature?
- What are the asset allocation restrictions with the Guaranteed Minimum Lifetime Withdrawal Benefit?

What is best for you depends upon your circumstances. Turn the page to learn what your next steps could be. This secret is not investment advice, but it is a suggestion that you should think about your retirement savings regularly.

65

You can now understand the Guaranteed Minimum Withdrawal Benefit.

(Continued from page 260)

On the opposite page, W.V.H.,Inc. created a hypothetical chart in order to evaluate the real benefit of the Guaranteed Minimum Withdrawal Benefit rider under an almost worst case scenario. They illustrated a $100,000 investment in a Variable Annuity with the Guaranteed Minimum Withdrawal Benefit rider with a gross portfolio return of 0% plus the 1% cost of the rider.

The income benefit base is the yardstick that measures how much income you can receive assuming no withdrawals. On the chart, there are two scenarios. The left side show withdrawals of $5,000 beginning in year 1 and the right side shows withdrawals of $7500 beginning in year 10. Their thought process was if the rider were beneficial to the annuity owner at a gross portfolio return of 0% plus the 1% cost of this rider, it would probably be more beneficial with a gross portfolio return of 8%. What is great about the chart is that you can select any year, read across, and see the rider's value or the lack of value.

If you start the withdrawals in the 10th year, your annual amount of withdrawal is $7,500, which is 5% of $150,000, the income benefit base. Some investors mistakenly think the 5% is a guaranteed return on their initial $100,000 investment. This is not the case. The $100,000 is not guaranteed either. Only a lifetime withdrawal amount is guaranteed.

You also need to understand how the withdrawals are made from your contract. The annual withdrawals are first deducted from your "annuity account value." For example, let's assume you make an initial investment of $100,000 and the Variable Annuity has a return like described above for the next 40 years. For this hypothetical example, and for simplicity, we will ignore the expense deductions except the cost of this rider. Naturally, there will be annual fees and expenses—fees and expenses clearly spelled out in the important prospectus and annuity literature.

(Continued on page 264)

Calculating The Value Of This Rider

Year	Income Benefit Base	Lifetime Withdrawal Benefit	Cumulative	Annuity Account Value	Cost of Rider	Cumulative	Income Benefit Base	Lifetime Withdrawal Benefit	Cumulative	Annuity Account Value	Cost of Rider	Cumulative
1	$100,000	$5,000	$5,000	$94,000	$1,000	$1,000	$105,000	0	0	$100,000	$1,050	$1,050
2	$100,000	$5,000	$10,000	$86,000	$1,000	$2,000	$110,000	0	0	$100,000	$1,100	$2,150
3	$100,000	$5,000	$15,000	$80,000	$1,000	$3,000	$115,000	0	0	$100,000	$1,150	$3,300
4	$100,000	$5,000	$20,000	$74,000	$1,000	$4,000	$120,000	0	0	$100000	$1,200	$4,500
5	$100,000	$5,000	$25,000	$68,000	$1,000	$5,000	$125,000	0	0	$100,000	$1,250	$6,250
6	$100,000	$5,000	$30,000	$62,000	$1,000	$6,000	$130,000	0	0	$100,000	$1,300	$7,550
7	$100,000	$5,000	$35,000	$56,000	$1,000	$7,000	$135,000	0	0	$100,000	$1,350	$8,900
8	$100,000	$5,000	$40,000	$50,000	$1,000	$8,000	$140,000	0	0	$100,000	$1,400	$10300
9	$100,000	$5,000	$45,000	$44,000	$1,000	$9,000	$145,000	0	0	$100,000	$1,450	$11,750
10	$100,000	$5,000	$50,000	$38,000	$1,000	$10,000	$150,000	$7,500	$7,500	$91,000	$1,500	$13,250
11	$100,000	$5,000	$55,000	$32,000	$1,000	$11,000	$150,000	$7,500	$15,000	$82,000	$1,500	$14,750
12	$100,000	$5,000	$60,000	$26,000	$1,000	$12,000	$150,000	$7,500	$22,500	$73,000	$1,500	$16,250
13	$100,000	$5,000	$65,000	$20,000	$1,000	$13,000	$150,000	$7,500	$30,000	$64,000	$1,500	$17,750
14	$100,000	$5,000	$70,000	$14,000	$1,000	$14,000	$150,000	$7,500	$37,500	$55,000	$1,500	$19,250
15	$100,000	$5,000	$75,000	$8,000	$1,000	$15,000	$150,000	$7,500	$45,000	$46,000	$1,500	$20,750
16	$100,000	$5,000	$80,000	$2,000	$1,000	$16,000	$150,000	$7,500	$52,500	$37,000	$1,500	$22,250
17	$100,000	$5,000	$85,000	0	0	$16,000	$150,000	$7,500	$60,000	$28,000	$1,500	$23,750
18	$100,000	$5,000	$90,000	0	0	$16,000	$150,000	$7,500	$67,500	$19,000	$1,500	$25,250
19	$100,000	$5,000	$95,000	0	0	$16,000	$150,000	$7,500	$75,000	$10,000	$1,500	$26,750
20	$100,000	$5,000	$100,000	0	0	$16,000	$150,000	$7,500	$82,500	$1,000	0	$28,250
21	$100,000	$5,000	$105,000	0	0	$16,000	$150,000	$7,500	$90,000	0	0	$28,250
22	$100,000	$5,000	$110,000	0	0	$16,000	$150,000	$7,500	$97,500	0	0	$28,250
23	$100,000	$5,000	$115,000	0	0	$16,000	$150,000	$7,500	$105,000	0	0	$28,250
24	$100,000	$5,000	$120,000	0	0	$16,000	$150,000	$7,500	$112,500	0	0	$28,250
25	$100,000	$5,000	$125,000	0	0	$16,000	$150,000	$7,500	$120,000	0	0	$28,250
26	$100,000	$5,000	$130,000	0	0	$16,000	$150,000	$7,500	$127,500	0	0	$28,250
27	$100,000	$5,000	$135,000	0	0	$16,000	$150,000	$7,500	$135,000	0	0	$28,250
28	$100,000	$5,000	$140,000	0	0	$16,000	$150,000	$7,500	$142,500	0	0	$28,250
29	$100,000	$5,000	$145,000	0	0	$16,000	$150,000	$7,500	$150,000	0	0	$28,250
30	$100,000	$5,000	$150,000	0	0	$16,000	$150,000	$7,500	$157,500	0	0	$28,250
31	$100,000	$5,000	$155,000	0	0	$16,000	$150,000	$7,500	$165,000	0	0	$28,250
32	$100,000	$5,000	$160,000	0	0	$16,000	$150,000	$7,500	$172,500	0	0	$28,250
33	$100,000	$5,000	$165,000	0	0	$16,000	$150,000	$7,500	$180,000	0	0	$28,250
34	$100,000	$5,000	$170,000	0	0	$16,000	$150,000	$7,500	$187,500	0	0	$28,250
35	$100,000	$5,000	$175,000	0	0	$16,000	$150,000	$7,500	$195,000	0	0	$28,250
36	$100,000	$5,000	$180,000	0	0	$16,000	$150,000	$7,500	$202,500	0	0	$28,250
37	$100,000	$5,000	$185,000	0	0	$16,000	$150,000	$7,500	$210,000	0	0	$28,250
38	$100,000	$5,000	$190,000	0	0	$16,000	$150,000	$7,500	$217,500	0	0	$28,250
39	$100,000	$5,000	$195,000	0	0	$16,000	$150,000	$7,500	$225,000	0	0	$28,250
40	$100,000	$5,000	$200,000	0	0	$16,000	$150,000	$7,500	$232,500	0	0	$28,250

This hypothetical chart assumes a gross 0% portfolio return plus the 1% cost of this rider.

Income Benefit Base = determines income you receive
Lifetime Withdrawal Benefit = annual withdrawal
Cumulative = total of lifetime withdrawal benefits

Annuity Account Value = what you or beneficiaries get
Cost of Rider = cost for this rider
Cumulative = total of amount deducted for this rider

What is best for you depends upon your circumstances. Turn the page to learn what your next steps could be. This secret is not investment advice, but it is a suggestion that you should think about your retirement savings regularly.

65

You can now understand the Guaranteed Minimum Withdrawal Benefit.

(Continued from page 262)

So let's assume you decide to start withdrawing your lifetime withdrawal benefit, for example, 5%, right away. Since 5% of $100,000, your annuity account value, is $5,000 and we are assuming a gross portfolio return of 0% plus the 1% cost of this rider, the account value is $94,000 at the end of year 1 because of the annual cost of the rider, $1,000, and the $5,000 annual withdrawal. After year 2, your account value is $88,000. After year 3, your account value is $82,000.

Finally, after 16 years of withdrawing $5,000 from the annuity account value, the insurance company in the 17th year must for the first time use its own money to pay the entire guaranteed lifetime withdrawal amount. Also, realize that after 17 years, there is no access to additional cash or possible inheritance.

Global conclusion: If you knew that gains were going to be 0%, you would not have purchased a Variable Annuity nor a mutual fund. If you knew you were going to die in the near future, you would not have purchased the rider either. However, the fact is that no one can predict the future, and purchasing this rider is really purchasing insurance in case you live too long, during a time when annual returns are disappointing.

Bottom Line: purchasing this rider may be a wise choice for some of your money depending upon your circumstances.

2 Potential Benefits

1) You can get a guaranteed lifetime income in spite of a poor market. 2) You can get guaranteed lifetime income and may leave an inheritance if there are market gains.

Next Steps

- If you are considering purchasing a Variable Annuity with a Guaranteed Minimum Lifetime Withdrawal Benefit, ask for some illustrations that project to age 90; with the following assumptions: 1) an average annual return of 8%, 2) an average annual return of 0%, 3) an average annual return that decreases 30% in year one and then has an average annual return increase of 5% for all the remaining years, and 4) an average annual return increase of 5% a year for 10 years followed by a decrease of 30% in year 11, followed by an average annual return increase of 5% for the remaining years.

  This will give you a sense for the value of the this rider in relation to its cost.

secret

66

The state you live in now or later can impact how much protection you have.

The guarantees in an annuity contract are as strong as the claims-paying ability of the insurer making the guarantees. However, there is a "state safety net" for owners and beneficiaries of annuity, life, and health contracts whose insurance companies become insolvent. Fortunately, insurance professionals are prohibited to bring this "state safety net" topic up and cannot use it in the solicitation of annuity, health, and life insurance. Turn the page to learn why we say "fortunately."

The state you live in now or later can impact how much protection you have.

A s you are aware, CDs can be FDIC insured. And, when an FDIC institution fails, the FDIC steps in and finds a "new buyer." Ideally, within hours or days, depositors can access their CD dollars. Without a doubt, the FDIC coverage, $250,000, and the speed that they have kept depositors whole is an advantage to owning a CD.

The question that you have to answer is whether you are paying too high of a price for the FDIC coverage. Arguably, we are always paying too much whenever we put all of our money in one place.

Annuities are NOT FDIC insured. But, their guarantees are as strong as the claims-paying ability of the insurer making the guarantees. Fortunately, there is a "state safety net" for owners and beneficiaries of annuity, life, and health contracts whose insurance companies become insolvent.

Simply put, every state has their own guaranty association designed to protect their state residents. Insurance companies licensed to do business in that state are required to be members of the guaranty association. When an insurer becomes insolvent, the state guaranty association obtains money from other members of the guaranty association so coverage, benefits, and claims can be paid.

Fortunately, insurance, and investment professionals are prohibited to bring this "safety net" topic up and use it in the solicitation of annuity and life insurance. Why do we imply that we are glad that the state guaranty association cannot be used to convey an extra layer of safety?

If you have a CD with the strongest bank and your brother has a CD with the weakest bank, your money and your brother's money are equally insured by the full faith of the government. With some degree of exaggeration, it almost does not matter where you have your CD as long it is a FDIC bank and it is within FDIC limits. With annuities, it does matter which insurance company has your money since coverage differs from state to state. Fortunately, there are many strong insurance companies.

States Protect Their Residents From Insurer Insolvency Differently

Resident Coverage

Some states offer coverage only for those who reside in that state at the time of the insurance insolvency. Do you know where you will live in 5, 10, 20 years?

Unallocated Annuity Contracts

There are thousands of pension plan participants in unallocated annuity contracts, some protected by the Federal Pension Benefit Guaranty Corporation. Some states expressly exclude unallocated annuity contracts from any coverage; other states protect them up to 5 million dollars. Do you know where you will be living in the future?

Individual Annuity Contracts vs. Group Annuity Contracts

Many states exclude coverage to non-residents who are a certificate holder (owner) of a group annuity contract. As a result, it is possible for a resident of the state to purchase a group annuity contract and see their coverage evaporate to zero when they move to another state.

Coverage

All states offer coverage to their residents for most types of Fixed Annuities of, at least, $100,000; California is unique in that coverage is 80% of the contract value for most types of Fixed Annuities with a $250,000 benefit level. In some states, coverage is increased to $300,000-$500,000 if the Fixed Annuity is in a payout status.

None of the above is bad news. The insurance industry does not have to replicate the FDIC insurance program. Their annuities have tax deferral. Their life insurance has a tax-free death benefit. Annuity payments are excluded from taxation to some extent. We are fortunate to have the coverage we have.

Bottom Line: The insurance companies' guarantees are as strong as the claims-paying ability of the insurer making the guarantees. Fortunately, there are many strong insurance companies out there.

Reach out to your state department of insurance and learn more about their guaranty association and their exclusions.

What is best for you depends upon your circumstances. Turn the page to learn what your next steps could be. This secret is not investment advice, but it is a suggestion that you should think about your retirement savings regularly.

All parties should see the insurer disclosure and annuity contract for guaranteed interest rates and values. Bank CDs are insured up to applicable limits by the FDIC. Annuities are insurance products and are NOT insured by the FDIC or any other federal government agency. The guarantees in an annuity contract are subject to the claims-paying ability of the insurer making the guarantees. Annuities have earnings which are taxable upon withdrawal and, if taken before age 59.5, may be subject to IRS penalties. Withdrawals taken during the Surrender Charge period above the penalty-free amount will be subject to Surrender Charges and a possible Market Value Adjustment.

The state you live in now or later can impact how much protection you have.

Next Steps

- Consult with your tax and legal advisors.

- Reach out to your state department of insurance and learn more about their guaranty association and their exclusions.

- Read what the independent rating agencies are saying about your insurance company.

- Ask your tax or legal advisors to review how your insurance company invests their assets, and the amount of money they have in capital and surplus.

- Diversify.

secret (67)

Surrender charges protect annuity owners from a "run on the bank."

Annuity owners often pay a surrender charge if they surrender or exchange their annuity during the surrender charge period. This can be an advantage since surrender charges protect the annuity carrier from a "run on the bank" and, as a result, increases the probability that the insurer remains strong. Turn the page to learn why you want a reasonable surrender charge.

67 Surrender charges protect annuity owners from a "run on the bank."

A surrender charge period is an insurance company's way of attempting to protect itself from "a run on the bank," in other words, protection from massive surrenders or excess withdrawals by annuity owners. Do you want your retirement money to be with an insurance company that is trying to protect itself from "a run on the bank" or with an insurance company that is not trying to protect itself?

In order for an insurance company to provide a guaranteed interest rate for the life of the annuity or a competitive guaranteed interest rate for one to ten years, the insurance company needs to purchase obligations like government and corporate bonds. However, when interest rates rise, the value of a bond goes down in value prior to the bond's maturity.

Imagine a hypothetical annuity without surrender charges paying a 5% interest rate. What would those annuity contract holders of that hypothetical annuity do in renewal years if other annuities were paying 10% interest and they were still getting 5%? The annuity contract holders would "surrender." In other words, "cash in" their annuity or exchange their annuity for another annuity paying that 10% interest rate.

In other words, there would be a "run on the bank "since there would be no surrender penalties holding them back from surrendering or exchanging their annuity. And, wouldn't those annuity contract holders expect to get 100% of their premium and 100% of their interest since our hypothetical annuity did not have a surrender charge period? However, it would be more difficult for the insurer to give 100% of the premium and earnings to many of their contract holders if some of the bonds supporting the insurance company guarantees were selling for 75 cents on the dollar. And, some of the bonds could be selling at 75 cents on a dollar in an increasing interest rate environment.

(Continued on page 272)

A surrender charge is an insurance company's way of protecting itself from a "run on the bank."

"Do you want your money to be with an institution that is trying to protect itself from a run on the bank, or from an institution that is not trying to protect itself from a run on the bank?"

Surrender charges protect annuity owners from a "run on the bank."

(Continued from page 270)

Above all, you must win.

That is why we ask:

"Where do you want some of your retirement money? Do you want some of your retirement money to be with an insurance company that is trying to protect itself from a run on the bank? Or, do you want some of your retirement money to be with an insurance company that is not trying to protect itself from a run on the bank?"

There must be three winners. The insurance company must win. Above all, you must win. And, if both of you win, then the insurance or investment professional wins too.

Next Steps

- Consult with your tax and legal advisors.

- Reach out to your insurance professional regarding products that can help you accumulate more money for retirement.

- Take cautious baby steps.

- Circle back to your tax and legal advisors regarding the products that you are considering to buy.

- Diversify.

- Understand and read what you are about to sign.

(68)

An excess withdrawal could cancel a major guarantee found in annuities.

*T*his secret was written by Scott Stolz, Senior Vice President, Private Client Group Investment Products, Raymond James Insurance Group; the views expressed in this secret are solely Scott's views and not necessarily the views of his company.* The lifetime income riders found in many Variable Annuities can potentially provide financial independence for some annuity owners since they can be assured of guaranteed lifetime income plus access to potentially more money if they ever need more. Understandably, insurer actuaries had to add other provisions in the annuity to make this benefit possible. Turn the page to learn more.

68

An excess withdrawal could cancel a major guarantee found in annuities.

Accessing lifetime income through a Variable Annuity living benefit can provide tremendous peace of mind for many retirees. You will sleep much better at night assured that your income will not only be paid no matter how long you live, but will also not decline no matter how poorly the market might perform. On top of that, if the market does well, you may actually experience an increase in your lifetime income payment. However, as the old saying goes, "there is no free lunch." To get these guarantees, you must follow the rules of the rider. Not following the rules can cost you dearly in terms of future income.

All Variable Annuity living benefits allow the policy owner to make annual withdrawals of a specific percentage of the income benefit base—typically 4-6% depending upon the age of the client when the first withdrawal is made. I have emphasized the words "first withdrawal" for a reason. The client brochure will often state that the income percentage is locked in when "income" starts. To a client, "income" typically means when he or she routinely accesses the annuity for income. It's not uncommon for a client to make a one time withdrawal from the annuity due to a need for funds. The client does not typically think of this as "income," but for the purposes of the rider, the insurance company does.

Once a withdrawal is made, it is very important that you do not exceed the allowable withdrawal in any contract year. Any such withdrawal will be deemed an excess withdrawal from the rider. The client brochure will typically state that "excess withdrawals may reduce the living and death benefits. See the prospectus for details." Those that take the time to actually read the prospectus will learn just how harmful an excess withdrawal can be—especially if the account value is below the income benefit base.

(Continued on page 276)

Depending upon your annuity contract, an excess withdrawal by you can affect your values 1 of 3 different ways. Bottom Line: Know how your annuity works or take withdrawals from other non-annuity assets.

Method #1: Income Benefit Base reduced by the amount of the excess withdrawal.

annuity Account Value: $80,000
Income Benefit Base: $110,000
5% Guaranteed Minimum Withdrawal Benefit(GMWB) allowed: $5,500
Actual withdrawal taken: $7,500
Amount of excess withdrawal: $2,000

Annuity Account Value after allowed 5% withdrawal: $80,000 - 5,500 = $74,500
% reduction in annuity account value due to excess: $2,000/$74,500 = 2.7%
Reduction in Income Benefit Base: $110,000 x (1-.027)= $107,300
New 5% GMWB withdrawal amount: $5,351

Method #2: Income Benefit Base reduced by the entire withdrawal

Annuity Account Value: $80,000
Income Benefit Base: $110,000
5% Guaranteed Minimum Withdrawal Benefit (GMWB) allowed: $5,500
Actual withdrawal taken: $7,500
Amount of excess: $2,000

% reduction in account value due to w/d: $7,500/$80,000 = 9.4%
Reduction in income benefit base: $110,000 x (1-.094)= $99,687
New 5% GMWB withdrawal amount: $4,984

Method #3: Income Benefit Base reduced to the lower of the account value after the withdrawal or the income benefit base less the amount of the withdrawal

Annuity Account Value: $80,000
Income Benefit Base: $110,000
5% Guaranteed Minimum Withdrawal Benefit (GMWB) allowed: $5,500
Actual withdrawal taken: $7,500
Amount of excess: $2,000

a) Account Value after withdrawal: $80,000 - $7,500 = $72,500
b) Previous Income Benefit Base less withdrawal: $110,000 - $7,500 = $102,500
c) New Income Benefit Base is lesser of a) or b): $72,500
d) New 5% GMWB withdrawal amount: $3,625

An excess withdrawal could cancel a major guarantee found in annuities.

(Continued from page 274)

Basically, there are 3 methods that insurance companies may use in calculating the effect of an excess withdrawal on future income payments due the policy owner. We provide an example on the previous page. You can see that even in the first example, an excess withdrawal of just $2,000 reduces the client's annual income for life by $149, or 7.5%. While this is not a terrible financial outcome, it does indicate that the client would be better, if possible, to take the extra $2,000 from other assets. In the second example, the extra $2,000 costs the client $516 per year for life. Clearly, unless the client has a relatively short life expectancy, this does not make much financial sense. But it's the last example that is catastrophic. By making an excess withdrawal when these rules are in place, the client resets the income benefit base to the account value. In affect, the client has paid for a living benefit that for all practical purposes, no longer exists. It is important that you take great care in avoiding the third situation. This situation has the affect of eliminating any benefits accrued to date by the rider. Fortunately, very few riders being sold today follow this method. However, as recently as 2008, I would not have been able to make such a statement.

One last word of warning: every Variable Annuity brochure will state that the policy owner can make a 10% "free withdrawal" each year. This withdrawal might be "free" of surrender charges, but can often create an excess withdrawal when it comes to the living benefit. It is not uncommon for annuity owners to confuse the two. It may never occur to them that a "free withdrawal" can actually reduce their allowable annual income.

Next Steps

- Consult with your tax and legal advisors.
- Reach out to your to your insurance professional for effective ways to receive guaranteed lifetime income while remaining invested.
- Understand how the annuity and the rider work.
- Take cautious baby steps.
- Circle back to your tax and legal advisors regarding the products that you are considering.
- Diversify.
- Read and understand what you are about to sign.

secret

69

Forget about recovering your losses quickly.

I n the 1990s, the stock market was kind to millions. It was not uncommon for some people to have received double digit gains. However, what goes up can go down and losses cannot be recovered easily. To learn what it takes to recover annual losses of 10%, 15%, and 20%, turn the page slowly. To learn how to avoid annual losses in the future, turn the page quickly.

Forget about recovering your losses quickly.

S ince some of you lost 30-50% of your money during the 2008 recession, let's examine what you need to recover those losses quickly.

On the opposite page, we show annual gains of 10% each year for three consecutive years. Since what goes up can also go down, we show a loss of 10% in year 4. In order to maintain an average annual gain of 10% for five years, you would need an annual gain of 35% in year five to make up for that 10% loss in year four. With annual gains of 15% for three years and a loss of 15% in year four, you would need an annual gain of 56% in year five to average 15% for five years. With annual gains of 20% for three consecutive years and a loss of 20% in year four, you would need a gain of 81% in year five to average 20% for those five years.

Since these high gains in year five might be too optimistic, wouldn't it be nice if you could eliminate that fourth year loss? With many Indexed Annuities, you can eliminate that fourth year loss. How? With some Indexed Annuities, interest can be credited in your annuity based on increases and decreases in an external index like the Dow Jones Industrial Average℠. Said differently, if the index increases, you can get a percentage of that increase credited to your annuity. If the index decreases, a 0% interest rate is credited in your annuity.

Would you like to get a percentage, for example, 50% or 60% of the increases in an index if you're guaranteed a 0% crediting rate in years that the index decreases?

To Recover Losses Quickly

Year	Gain or (Loss)
1	10%
2	10%
3	10%
4	(-10%)
5	35%
5 year average accumulation rate:10%	

Year	Gain or (Loss)
1	15%
2	15%
3	15%
4	(-15%)
5	56%
5 year average accumulation rate:15%	

Year	Gain or (Loss)
1	20%
2	20%
3	20%
4	(-20%)
5	81%
5 year average accumulation rate:20%	

All parties should see the insurer disclosure and annuity contract for guaranteed interest rates and values. Bank CDs are insured up to applicable limits by the FDIC. Annuities are NOT insured by the FDIC or any other agency and are subject to investment risks, including the possible loss of principal. The guarantees in an annuity contract are subject to the claims-paying ability of the insurer making the guarantees. Annuities have earnings which are taxable upon withdrawal and, if taken before age 59.5, may be subject to a 10% Federal early withdrawal penalty. Annuities can have a surrender charge period of 10 years or more and a possible Market Value Adjustment. Naturally, the above charts are hypothetical, and the charts do not represent any specific investment or insurance product.

Forget about recovering your losses quickly.

Next Steps

- Consult with your tax and legal advisors.

- Reach out to your insurance professional regarding products that can lessen the probability of losses.

- Take cautious baby steps.

- Circle back to your tax and legal advisors regarding the products that you are considering buying.

- Diversify.

- Understand and read what you are about to sign.

Smart people select insurance companies to insure everything important to them.

T oo many think they are "insurance poor" since they are paying premiums to a wide variety of insurers for all kinds of insurance protection. However, many find out that they are, in actuality, "insurance rich" when an important asset disappears or is lost or damaged. Turn the page to see if you are insurance rich or insurance poor.

Smart people select insurance companies to insure everything important to them.

W e select insurance companies to insure our single most valuable asset, our $200,000 home, our $500,000 home, or our $1,000,000 home. We select insurance companies to insure our cars. We select insurance companies to insure our jewelry. We select an insurance company to insure our ability to bring home a paycheck each week, disability income. We select an insurance company to insure our health and our lives. And, we select insurance companies to stand behind the dollars that we have in our annuities.

Isn't it comforting to know that the claims-paying ability of strong, well-respected insurance companies can stand behind your home, your car, your jewelry, your paycheck, your life, your health, and your annuity?

The bottom line is that the guarantees made in an annuity contract are as strong as the claims-paying ability of the insurance company making the guarantees. And fortunately, some of the strongest insurance companies in the industry offer annuities.

The Assets That Consumers Ask Insurance Companies To Insure Or Protect

1. Home

2. Car

3. Jewelry

4. Life

5. Health

6. Retirement

All parties should see the insurer disclosure and annuity contract for guaranteed interest rates and values. Bank CDs are insured up to applicable limits by the FDIC. Annuities are insurance products and are NOT insured by the FDIC or any other federal government agency. The guarantees in an annuity contract are subject to the claims-paying ability of the insurer making the guarantees. Annuities have earnings which are taxable upon withdrawal and, if taken before age 59.5, may be subject to IRS penalties. Withdrawals taken during the Surrender Charge period above the penalty-free amount will be subject to Surrender Charges and a possible Market Value Adjustment.

Smart people select insurance companies to insure everything important to them.

Next Steps

- See what the independent rating services such as A.M. Best, Standard & Poors®, Moody's, Weiss and Fitch are saying about the insurance company you are considering.

- Ask your tax and legal advisors to look at their investments and their capital and surplus.

- Reach out to your insurance professional.

- Diversify.

Your annuity can credit interest based on a percentage of gains in a well-known index.

Indexed Annuities can offer interest potentially higher than Certificates of Deposit and Traditional Fixed Annuities since interest is credited based on changes in well-known indexes. And, if that were not enough, Indexed Annuities guarantee a minimum value in excess of your premium at the end of the term just in case there are negative changes in the index. Turn the page if you want to learn about the product that so many are talking about today.

71

Your annuity can credit interest based on a percentage of gains in a well-known index.

In 1995, Indexed Annuities—as we know them today—were unveiled to the public. To the best of our knowledge, no new insurance product has ever gained the sales momentum that Indexed Annuities did during its first 15 years. Unfortunately, it may also be the most misunderstood insurance product in the financial services industry. While it may not be the best product for all people, Indexed Annuities can be an effective product for so many. Is the Indexed Annuity an effective product for you? Surprisingly, that question is easier to answer after we learn what an Indexed Annuity is not.

In the opinion of many, the Indexed Annuity is not a security since the insurer issuing the annuity contract guarantees a minimum guaranteed value at the end of the term; said differently, at the end of the surrender charge period, you are guaranteed to have your initial premium intact plus interest (assuming no withdrawals). The interest is a result of the insurer crediting interest at a rate based on the change in an index during the crediting period. And again unlike a security, the owners of many Indexed Annuities are credited a 0% interest rate when the index had a negative change from one year to the next.

In fact, we show on the opposite page, an example to how one hypothetical Indexed Annuity accumulated more money over the past 13 years compared to a well-known index during a Bear Market, then double digit returns in 2009 and 2010 then a small single digit increase in 2011 and 2012 and a 25% gain in 2013. Naturally during a Bull Market when the market is going up and up and up, the well-known-index would be higher than the Indexed Annuity. Said differently, an Indexed Annuity is not supposed to out-perform the stock market. It is designed to give you a percentage of the gains. As a result, the Indexed Annuity can potentially credit interest higher than Traditional Fixed Annuities and Certificates of Deposit.

(Continued on page 288)

How An Indexed Annuity Can Compare To A Well-Known Index

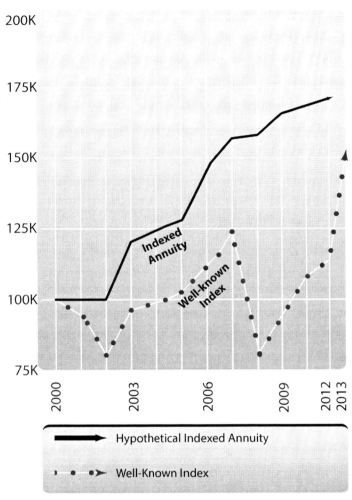

Hypothetical Indexed Annuity

Well-Known Index

What is best for you depends upon your circumstances. Turn the page to learn what your next steps could be. This secret is not investment advice, but it is a suggestion that you should think about your retirement savings regularly.

Your annuity can credit interest based on a percentage of gains in a well-known index.

(Continued from page 286)

Indexed Annuities are not FDIC insured like CDs. In return, you receive benefits not found in CDs such as tax-deferred accumulation, the option to elect guaranteed monthly income for life, and a guaranteed minimum value for the life of the policy. On the opposite page, we show how the guaranteed minimum value accumulates each year regardless of index increases and decreases.

As a result, you get potentially more money later, a guaranteed minimum annuity value for any point of time, and the protection that you will not outlive your money. Plus, since you have chosen insurance companies to insure your life, health, cars, and homes, it makes sense that you should again turn to a strong insurance company to stand behind your retirement dollars.

The Indexed Annuity is not as liquid as a short term Certificate of Deposit or Money Market account. Indexed Annuities need to have a surrender charge period of 7-10 years or longer so the insurer can invest properly, compete, and protect itself from a run on the bank. (See Secret 67). This surrender charge period also serves as a reminder that tax-deferred status has been extended to Tax-Deferred Annuities as a way for you to save for a long-term need, retirement. The Indexed Annuity is not the first place you turn to when you need money for life's surprises and emergencies. Instead, you turn to taxable short term FDIC accounts.

Since we have just examined what an Indexed Annuity is NOT, let's examine what an Indexed Annuity is. An Indexed Annuity is the only product that gives you tax-deferred accumulation, the option to elect guaranteed monthly income, a guaranteed minimum value for the life of the policy, and the crediting of interest based on changes in an external index; if the index increases, you get some stated percentage of that increase 100% with cap and or fee; if the index decreases, you can get 0% interest credited depending upon the type of Indexed Annuity you own.

(Continued on page 290)

How The Guaranteed Minimum Value Adds Extra Protection

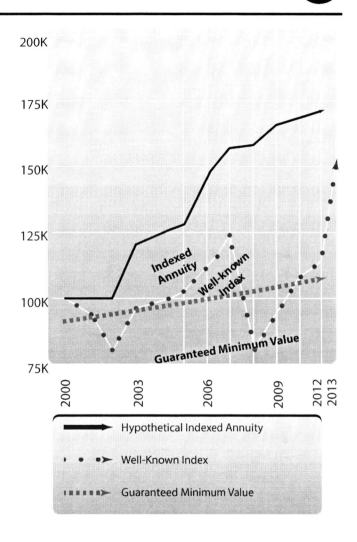

Legend:
- Hypothetical Indexed Annuity
- Well-Known Index
- Guaranteed Minimum Value

What is best for you depends upon your circumstances. Turn the page to learn what your next steps could be. This secret is not investment advice, but it is a suggestion that you should think about your retirement savings regularly.

71

Your annuity can credit interest based on a percentage of gains in a well-known index.

(Continued from page 288)

In summary, the Indexed Annuity can be a nice addition when you want to diversify your money among a variety of products that can collectively protect you, to some extent, from interest rate risk, market risk, inflation risk, and the risk of outliving your money. The Indexed Annuity is not a product for all people, all of the time. However, it can be a great product for some people.

Next Steps

- Consult with your tax and legal advisors.

- Reach out to your insurance professional and ask them the following;

    Is an Indexed Annuity suitable for you?

    If so, what is guaranteed and what is not guaranteed in the Indexed Annuity being considered?

    What is the participation rate, cap, spread and fees, if any?

    What is the surrender charge period and is there a market value adjustment?

    Ask how the withdrawal features and the death benefit work.

    Ask to see a history of interest rates credited by the insurance company for their Indexed Annuities. While the past is not an indication of the future; you are trying to find a pattern of fairness from the insurer to the policyholder.

- Circle back to your tax and legal advisors regarding the products that you are considering to buy.

- Take cautious baby steps.

- Diversify.

- Understand and read what you are about to sign.

secret 72

Annuity owners appear to be smart, contented and happily married.

In this author's opinion, annuity owners appear to be smart, contented and even (smile) happily married. In 2013, individual annuity contract owners were surveyed. Some of the results are published on the following pages. If you are already an annuity owner, simply turn the page to see if you fall into the definition of a typical annuity owner. If you are NOT an owner yet, turn to page 292 to see if you want to be part of the "Annuity Family".

Annuity owners appear to be smart, contented and happily married.

Individual Annuity Contract Owners

- 86% of individual annuity owners cite the tax treatment of individual annuities as important in their decision

- The average age at which a individual annuity contract purchaser purchased their first annuity was 51

- 39% made their first purchase before the age of 50

- The average age of a current individual annuity contract owner is age 70

Individual Annuity Owners: Marital Status

- 58% are married
- 24% are widowed
- 10% were never married
- Only 7% were divorced

Individual Annuity Owners: Education

- 53% have graduated from college; 26% have completed at least some post college graduate work

Individual Annuity Owners: Miscellaneous

- Almost half (45%) who are already retired have withdrawn money; 33% of them have begun receiving periodic payments

- 33% of retired owners of variable annuities with Guaranteed Lifetime Withdrawal benefits have already begun taking lifetime withdrawals

Source:The Committee of Annuity Insurers, Survey of Owners of Individual Annuity Contracts (The Gallup Organization and Matthew Greenwald & Associates, 2013)

Individual Annuity Contract Owners

34% are professionals like doctors, lawyers, and teachers; 15% are business owners or company executives

90% indicated that a "safe purchase" was important in their annuity buying decision

87% agree that the insurance or investment guarantees were an important aspect to buying an individual annuity

87% expect to use their individual annuity as a financial cushion in case they live beyond life expectancy

Close to 90% considered the Guaranteed Lifetime Withdrawal Benefit as a valuable provision; 48% very valuable

15% have already withdrawn money from their annuity via partial withdrawals; 27% on a periodic basis

58% report that the current value of their annuity is $100,000 or more, including one-third who say it is at least $200.000

59% report that the used existing savings to fund their annuity purchase; 40% used investment proceeds(please note that owners were allowed to chose multiple sources as their source to fund an annuity)

70% view their annuity savings as a financial resource to avoid being a burden to their children; 73% view their annuity purchase as an emergency fund in case of a catastrophic illness or nursing home care

79% also have IRAs; 69% also own mutual funds, 58% cash value life insurance, 58% individual stocks and bonds, and 41% certificates of deposit (CDs); in 2009, 58% owned CDs

34% never participated in a retirement program offered through their employer

Owners who have NOT graduated from college are more likely to have never participated in an employer plan than owners who earned a college degree (46%-26%)

Source:The Committee of Annuity Insurers, Survey of Owners of Individual Annuity Contracts (The Gallup Organization and Matthew Greenwald & Associates, 2013)

Annuity owners appear to be smart, contented and happily married.

Next Steps

- Consult with your tax and legal advisors.

- Take cautious baby steps.

- Circle back to your tax and legal advisors regarding the products that you are considering.

- Diversify.

- Understand and read what you are about to sign.

secret

The cost of having all of your money at FDIC insured banks can be very expensive.

The cost of having all of your money in any one place can be very expensive. However, the cost of having all of your money in a FDIC insured bank is easy to calculate since all you need to know is your tax bracket and the interest rates for the CDs. To figure out what you are implicitly paying for an important layer of FDIC protection, go to the next page.

73

The cost of having all of your money at FDIC insured banks can be very expensive.

Not too long ago, a man stopped me following one of my speaking engagements and asked me if there were any tax-deferred products that also had FDIC insurance.

The words below and the chart on the opposite page describe the dialogue between the two of us:

> Man: "Mr. Harris, the annuity sounded awfully good. Is it insured by the government?"
>
> Me: "No, it is not but if I could arrange FDIC insurance for your annuity, you would be interested, wouldn't you?"
>
> Man: He smiled, moved very close to me, and replied, "Yes."
>
> Me: "Would you still be interested if I could provide FDIC insurance and it only required a small annual premium from you each year?"
>
> Man: "Heck, no!"
>
> Me: "With all due respect, in a way you are already paying an annual premium for FDIC coverage. For every $100,000 you have in the bank, you are earning $5,000 in interest. However, 28% of your interest, $1,400, is going to the government each year in income taxes. In return, the government insures your money. Over the next ten years, you will pay $14,000 to the government in income taxes. In return, they insured your money. Sir, FDIC is nice, but paying $1400 for 10 years adds up to $14,000, that is over $3,000 per initial, F.D.I.C."
>
> Man: "That's too expensive!"

Friends, having all or most of your money in FDIC insured CDs or in any product including an annuity can be too expensive.

Taxes Paid To IRS Over 10 Years

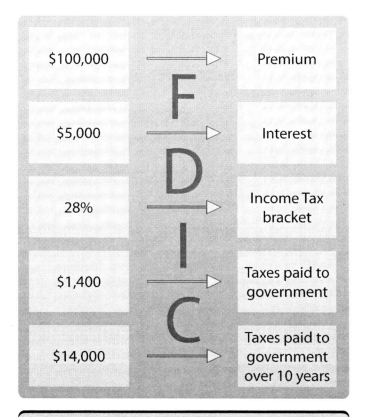

$100,000	⟹	Premium
$5,000	⟹	Interest
28%	⟹	Income Tax bracket
$1,400	⟹	Taxes paid to government
$14,000	⟹	Taxes paid to government over 10 years

This hypothetical example assumes a $100,000 premium, a 5% interest rate, a 28% tax bracket, and is for illustrative purposes only. Bank CDs are insured up to applicable limits by the FDIC. Annuities are insurance products and are NOT insured by the FDIC or any other federal government agency. The guarantees in an annuity contract are subject to the claims-paying ability of the insurer making the guarantees. Annuities have earnings which are taxable upon withdrawal and, if taken before age 59.5, may be subject to IRS penalties. Withdrawals taken during the Surrender Charge period above the penalty-free amount will be subject to Surrender Charges and a possible Market Value Adjustment.

73 *The cost of having all of your money at FDIC insured banks can be very expensive.*

Next Steps

- Diversify.

- Know your tolerance for risk and time horizon, in other words, how much time before you need all or some of your money.

- Keep at least 6 month's income in highly liquid FDIC insured accounts like 30-90 day CDs.

- Consult with your tax and legal advisors.

- Reach out to your insurance professional.

- Act cautiously and take baby steps.

secret

An annuity crediting 4% interest is like a bank paying 5.55% interest.

While there is no hard proof that he said it, Albert Einstein is often attributed with saying that the 8th wonder of the world was "compound interest." You might agree when you turn the page and discover an easy way to compare the accumulation power of Tax-Deferred Annuities to taxable alternatives like CDs.

74

An annuity crediting 4% interest is like a bank paying 5.55% interest.

T

he power of tax deferral can be illustrated and presented in a wide variety of ways and using taxable equivalent yields is one way if it is done correctly. It is unfair to say that an annuity crediting a 4% interest rate is equivalent to a Certificate of Deposit paying 5.55% interest since you eventually pay income taxes on the tax-deferred interest. What is fair is showing what kind of taxable equivalent yield you would need from a Certificate of Deposit in order to accumulate the same amount of money as an annuity. For example, let's assume we have $100,000 going into a hypothetical annuity crediting 4% interest. In five short years, the annuity value is $121,665. Assuming a 28% federal tax bracket, you would need 5.55% interest in a Certificate of Deposit to accumulate the same amount of money as the annuity. Now, let's learn how to do this calculation using easy math.

To calculate the interest rate that you would need from a CD to accumulate the same amount of money as a tax-deferred annuity:

1. Simply subtract your combined tax bracket, state and federal, from 100. So if you are in a combined tax bracket of 28%, 28% minus 100 is 72, correct? That number you get after subtraction is what you keep after taxes.

2. Now divide that number, what you keep after taxes, like 72 into the interest rate that the annuity is crediting. And, when you divide 72 into the 4% interest, the annuity crediting interest rate, you get 5.55% interest. And that is the interest rate you would need from a CD to accumulate the same amount of money as an annuity.

A Homework Assignment:

Assume that a) you have three brothers who are in combined tax brackets of 15%, 36%, and 46% respectively, and b) they all can get a hypothetical annuity interest rate of 4%. Please calculate what they would need in a CD to accumulate the same amount of money as a Tax-Deferred Annuity. To grade yourself, look at the chart on the previous page to see if you deserve a gold star from your family.

The Taxable Yield You Would Need To Accumulate The Same Amount Of Money As An Annuity

	Tax-Deferred Fixed Annuity Interest Rate				
TB*	4%	5%	6%	7%	8%
15%	4.71%	5.88%	7.06%	8.24%	9.41%
28%	5.55%	6.94%	8.33%	9.72%	11.11%
31%	5.80%	7.25%	8.70%	10.14%	11.59%
33%	5.97%	7.46%	8.96%	10.45%	11.94%
36%	6.25%	7.81%	9.38%	10.94%	12.50%
39%	6.56%	8.20%	9.84%	11.48%	13.11%
46%	7.41%	9.26%	11.11%	12.96%	14.81%

The above is hypothetical. Interest rates and returns do not stay level for long periods of time. Some products have fees, expenses, and risks. As a result, losses are possible with some products. This secret is not intended to provide investment advice, but it is a suggestion that you should think about your retirement savings regularly. Turn the page to learn what your next steps could be.

*Tax Bracket

W.V.H., Inc., its employees, officers, directors are not qualified to provide tax or legal advice.

An annuity crediting 4% interest is like a bank paying 5.55% interest.

Next Steps

- Consult with your tax and legal advisors.

- Reach out to your insurance professional regarding products that can help you accumulate more money.

- Take cautious baby steps.

- Circle back to your tax and legal advisors regarding the products that you are considering buying.

- Diversify.

- Understand and read what you are about to sign.

Taking Annuity Steps picks up where CD & Annuity Laddering leaves off.

J ust imagine a concept where you get tax deferral, protection from decreasing interest rates, and possible increasing interest rates. If that were not enough, you also get insurer penalty-free access to 100% of your money far earlier than you ever imagined. Just turn the page to learn more.

Taking Annuity Steps picks up where CD & Annuity Laddering leaves off.

If you liked CD Laddering in Secret 3, you will love this concept because you get tax-deferred interest instead of taxable interest. This is all possible because of our new patent-pending asset, Taking Annuity Steps, since 3 special newly written paragraphs added to the annuity contract by the annuity carrier will give you more benefits than you ever thought possible. When this edition of the book was written, insurance companies had just begun looking at our new words and our illustration system. We trust that Taking Annuity Steps will go into effect in 2011.

On the opposite page, we show $33,333 in 3 interest rate guarantee periods: 8, 9, and 10 years. At the end of the 8th year, you can surrender the $45,000 or exchange the $45,000 for another annuity with another insurer or renew the $45,000 with the same insurer. You might think that we are talking about the Annuity Laddering concept that has been around for some time. We are not. We are talking about Taking Annuity Steps which eliminates all of the disadvantages of traditional Annuity Laddering. First of all, with traditional Annuity Laddering, you never had access to all of your money at one time since only some of your money was coming out of the surrender charge period.

With Taking Annuity Steps, annuity owners can arrange for all of their money to "mature", in other words, for all of their money to be out of the surrender charge period at the same time since an annuity owner may select among a wide variety of interest rate guarantees within the same annuity contract. Plus, at the end of each guarantee period, the annuity owner may renew for 1-10 years. This simple provision to allow for renewals, especially short term renewals of 1-4 years allows the annuity owner to have insurer penalty free access to 100% of their money at the same time.

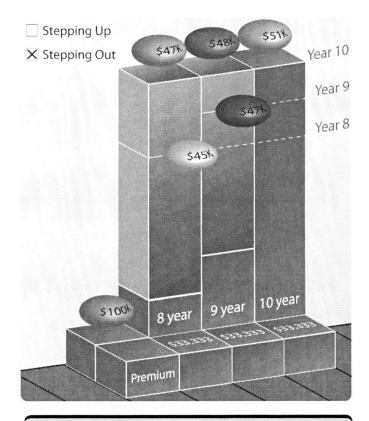

☐ Stepping Up

☒ Stepping Out

Year 10

Year 9

Year 8

$47K $48K $51K

$47K

$45K

$100K

8 year 9 year 10 year

$33,333 $33,333 $33,333

Premium

The interest rates for the Tax-Deferred Fixed Annuity are hypothetical since interest rates vary by product and carrier. All parties should see the insurer disclosure and annuity contract for guaranteed interest rates and values. This hypothetical example assumes a $100,000 premium, interest rates of 3.75% (8 year), 4% (9 year), 4.25% (10 year), a 28% tax bracket, and is for illustrative purposes only. Bank CDs are insured up to applicable limits by the FDIC. Annuities are insurance products and are NOT insured by the FDIC or any other federal government agency. The guarantees in an annuity contract are subject to the claims-paying ability of the insurer making the guarantees. Annuities have earnings which are taxable upon withdrawal and, if taken before age 59.5, may be subject to IRS penalties. Withdrawals taken during the Surrender Charge period above the penalty-free amount will be subject to Surrender Charges and a possible Market Value Adjustment.

75

Taking Annuity Steps picks up where CD & Annuity Laddering leaves off.

When you renew some of your annuity dollars for 1-4 years, is this extra liquidity in your best interest? No and yes! Disadvantage: Since the price you pay for liquidity is often measured in the interest rate, the interest rates that you get with shorter interest rate guarantee periods are often lower than interest rate guarantee periods of 8, 9, and 10 years. Advantage: For the first time ever, you'll be able to arrange for all of your dollars to be accessible at the same time without any insurance company penalty.

Advantages

Tax Deferral: Why pay taxes on all of your bank interest when you do not yet need the bank interest for income?

Lifetime Income: Annuities are the only financial product that give you a choice to elect lifetime income later.

Liquidity: *With Taking Annuity Steps,* you can get insurer penalty-free access to all of your money at almost any time by selecting the right interest rate guarantees during renewal years.

Increasing interest rates: Your annuity carrier or another insurer are more apt to offer you higher interest rates at renewal in year 1, 2, and 3 if interest rates are then higher.

Disadvantages

Since annuities purchased in the same calendar year with the same insurer would be "aggregated" for tax reporting purposes, withdrawing/surrendering money at the end of one interest rate guarantee period will result in the tax-deferred interest in the other interest rate guarantee periods to also be taxable.

Please consult with your tax advisor on the steps you must follow to keep a partial exchange a tax-free exchange.

Not all insurers allow for partial exchanges and some do not accept partial exchanges.

There are federal tax penalties for surrenders and withdrawals prior to age 59.5.

Next Steps

- Consult with your tax and legal advisors.
- Reach out to your insurance and investment professionals.
- Circle back with your tax or legal advisors regarding any product you are about to buy.

30 Short Bonus Secrets

You thought you were getting *75 Secrets* in this book. You are actually getting *105 Secrets* instead. It is W.V.H., Inc.,'s way of "under promising" and "over delivering." So many of you will really enjoy these *30 Short Bonus Secrets* since you will be able to learn in 30 minutes what took others a lifetime to learn.

Certificates of Deposit

1. You can find out if your bank is an FDIC insured bank.

There are two simple ways to double check to see if your bank is a FDIC insured bank. You can visit www.FDIC.gov/bankfind or you can call 1-877-ASK-FDIC.

2. You can find out how strong your bank is for free.

To find out how strong your bank is, go to www.bankrate.com. They give one to five star ratings on the financial strength of banks, savings institutions and credit unions. To find out if your bank has failed, go to www.fdic.gov. Remember, no bank customer has ever lost a single penny of insured deposits. However, not all deposits are insured.

3. It is easy to shop for the highest interest rates and lowest penalties for CDs.

If you visit www.bankrate.com, you will be able to get the highest interest rates for CDs from either national and local banks for almost every term from 30 days to 5 years and sometimes longer terms as long as 10 years. You can also "dig deeper" to see their penalties and compare their penalties to other banks as well. The USA Today, Wall Street Journal, and New York Times publish a short list of the Highest Yielding CDs regularly. With that being said, there is more to life than the highest interest rate since the trust and rapport that you have with your local bank representative can compound other advantages.

4. Some Certificates of Deposit can be terminated by the bank if interest rates decrease.

Callable CDs give the issuing bank the right to terminate the CD after a set period of time, but their reserved right is not mutual. If the bank calls or redeems your CD, you should receive the full amount of your original deposit plus any unpaid accrued interest. Ask your banker or broker if your CD is callable. If it is, "locking in" an interest rate in case interest rates go lower may not be a major benefit if the bank can "call" your CD anyway.

5. You can defer income taxes on your CD interest.

If you feel that you will be in a lower tax bracket next year, you can open a Certificate of Deposit that matures next year. Tell the bank representative that you want the interest to be paid at maturity, in other words, in the next tax year. There is a big difference between losing 28% of your bank interest to income taxes vs. losing 15% of your bank interest to income taxes. Said differently, if you purchase a CD in May, get a 9 month CD and ask for the interest to be paid at maturity, in February.

6. You can easily find out if your CD is FDIC insured.

On the FDIC's web site, there is an FDIC estimator that can help you stay within FDIC limits. It is called the Electronic Deposit Insurance Estimator (EDIE). Simply create a list of your deposit accounts for each bank and how they are owned such as single, joint, IRAs, revocable trust, etc.

Retirement

7. The best time to retire is not between the ages 62-66.

Unfortunately, too many think that retiring begins at a special age like at age 62 or 65 or 66. Nothing could be further from the truth. Retiring should begin at one or more of the following milestones: 1) when you have enough money to retire 2) when working no longer gives you the zest, confidence, and the strut in your walk that working once gave you, 3) when you no longer have your health, 4) when your spouse needs you 5) or when your adult children no longer financially need you for some of their events like a new home, unemployment, or your grandchildren's education or marriage.

8. Reduce your credit card debt as soon as possible.

Do you owe $2,000 to a credit card company and are you paying them 20% or 22% interest or more? If so, we would like you to go to the bank. Strike that. We would like you to run to the bank and get that $2,000 that is earning a whopping 1% interest at the bank and pay off that $2,000 of credit card debt. If you do, you will be 19% or 21% richer. However, from this point on, you should ask yourself "Do I need this or do I just want this" before handing your credit card over. Said differently, have you ever bought anything on sale and used your credit card to buy it? If so, did you really get it on sale or did you pay 22% more than you should have? In other words, spend less and save more for your retirement.

9. The cost of having all your money in one place can be real expensive.

The last few years taught us many things and having all of our money with one investment house, bank, money market fund, insurer or all of our 401(k) money in your company stock resulted in too many sleepless nights and many times a lot less money. When your Dad and Mom said, "Never put all of your eggs in one basket," they were right, again.

10. You need only 60-70% of your pre-retirement paycheck if you die soon; otherwise, you need 100%.

You might only need 60-70% of your pre-retirement paycheck during retirement if you don't live too long. However, when you consider your life expectancy, medical and insurance costs ramping up every year, inflation always returning, and higher federal and state income taxes around the corner, you will need 100% or more of your pre-retirement income during most of your retirement.

11. Social Security only replaces 40% of your pre-retirement income.

Generally speaking, the average monthly payment that a Social Security recipient receives is 40%[1] of what they were making before retirement. In order to make up for the difference, retirees rely on their savings, their pension plan, if any, return to the work force either part time or full time, or change how they live, entertain, and relax.

[1]Source: Social Security Administration.

12. You can now compare the performance and the fees in your 401(k) plan to over 5,000 other 401(k) plans.

There are companies who can compare your 401(k)to more than 5,000 other 401(k) plans covering over 20 million participants. BrightScope™ in San Diego, CA is one of the companies that can provide this service.

Give them a try. We just visited their website, www. brightscope.com this morning. We entered one of our client's names and in 10 seconds saw that my client had over $17,500,000 in 401(k) assets, an average account balance of $44,000, 410 participants and that they were above average in salary deferrals. We then registered for free to see how their fees compared to other 401(k) plans.

13. A divorcee can claim the Social Security benefits of their former spouse[1].

A deceased worker's former spouse age 62 or older may qualify for benefits if marriage lasted 10 years or more, is unmarried is not entitled to a higher Social Security benefit on his or her record, and if former spouse died fully insured. If former spouse was not fully insured at death, Social Security Administration for qualifications.

14. Employees are not taking advantage of the tax incentives they have at work to save.

The average percentage of pre-tax deferral among non-highly compensated participants in pension plans in 2008 was only

[1] Source: the Social Security Website, Survivors Benefits/Frequently Asked Questions

5.5%.[1] In spite of the advantages of being able to defer income taxes on wages deferred, getting tax-deferred accumulation, being 100% vested, so many employees are overlooking one of the easiest ways to save at work. Why? Some families think they need 100% of their take home pay but do they really need 100%? Step 1 Create priorities. How important is it for you to have a comfortable retirement? Would you rather have 2 front row tickets to a Bruce Springsteen concert now or 4 front row tickets to the Jonas Brothers' final performance later? Said differently, how much of a priority is where you live, how you live and who else lives with you during retirement? If financial and emotional independence is a top priority, tighten your belt. Have fewer dinners at sit down restaurants. Netflix movies instead of the local multiplex movie theater. And, certainly, ask yourself every time you have a credit card in your hand, "Do I need this thing I am about to buy or do I just want this thing?"

15. Greed is how consumers make their biggest financial mistake.

If you were to ask any group of people to explain the biggest, dumbest, and the worst investment or saving decision they ever made in their lifetime, you would find that greed was the villain almost every time. They were trying to get the absolute highest rate, lowest premium, or largest tax deduction. In return, they got disappointment, and the worst decision they ever made.

[1] Source: The Profit Sharing/401(k) Council of America's 52nd Annual Survey of Profit Sharing and 401(k) Plans: Reflecting 2008 Plan Experience

16. 93% of large 401(k) plans allow their participants to borrow.

According to the Employee Benefit Research Institute, 93% of the 401(k) plans that have more than 10,000 participants include a loan provision for their participants compared to 34% of the plans with 10 or fewer employees.[1]

In 2011, 21% of all 401(k) participants eligible for loans had a loan outstanding against the 401(k) account.[1]

In most instances, you can borrow either $50,000 or 50% of your vested assets, whichever is less. The loan must be paid in full within 5 years by making regular payments of principal and interest such as quarterly. The interest you pay does not go to a bank but is credited to your 401(k), and the processing fees for borrowing are quite low.

In spite of all of those advantages, borrowing from your retirement plan can dramatically affect how much money you have at retirement and can trigger a taxable event plus tax penalties if you do not repay the loan within 5 years. More seriously, the loan must be repaid within 60 days if you terminate employment or if they terminate employment.

17. 2000-2009 was the worst decade ever for the stock market.

According to the Yale School of Management International Center for Finance, the S&P 500® Total Return Index had a decade return of -0.32% per year cumulative annualized return. This was the worst decade loss ever.

[1] Source: EBRI issue brief number 390, December, 2012

Tax-Deferred Annuities

18. An insurance company's promises in an annuity contract are as strong as the insurance company making the promises.

Your annuity carrier can be strong or it can have a big parent or your state can provide coverage to policyholders of insolvent insurance companies. However, things can change. Simply put, the guarantees that an insurer makes are as strong as the claims-paying ability of that insurer making the guarantees. Fortunately, the insurance industry has a lot of strong insurers.

19. You can get 3% interest or more guaranteed for 1 year, 5 years, or for LIFE.

There are single premium and flexible premium annuities. Unlike single premium annuities, some flexible premium annuities can allow you to make contributions (premiums) almost whenever you wish. Depending upon the flexible premium annuity, the surrender charges do not reappear, or reappear for as short as one year or reappear for a period of years after you make the new contribution. Both types of annuities have a minimum guaranteed interest rate for the life of the policy. Said differently, no matter how low interest rates decrease elsewhere, the insurer MUST pay you, at least, it's minimum guaranteed interest rate.

So, if you already own a flexible premium annuity, you might be able to add more money to it and get a 3% minimum guaranteed interest rate. In fact, if you bought a

(Continued on page 316)

(Continued from page 315)

flexible premium annuity before 1997, the minimum guaranteed interest rate might be as high as 6%. Would you like no less than 3% or 6% interest for the life of the policy plus tax deferral plus the choice to elect guaranteed monthly income for as long as you live? If so, ask your insurance/investment professional to see if you own a flexible premium annuity.

20. The issue date of your annuity will determine if your withdrawals can be income tax free.

When an owner of an annuity withdraws money from their non-qualified annuity, the tax-deferred interest comes out first and it is taxable. It is only after all of the interest is withdrawn that the premium can be withdrawn income tax free. However, if you purchased an annuity before August 14, 1982, premium, not interest, could be withdrawn income tax-free first. Reach out to your tax advisor to see if your annuity was grandfathered* when this tax change was made in 1982.

21. Every product has a surrender penalty of some kind.

With Certificates of Deposit, we have penalties for premature surrender. In other words, loss of interest. With your home, the potential penalties would be the housing market when you attempt to sell the house. With securities, the selling price is what others are willing to pay. With Fixed and Variable Annuities, there is a surrender charge period. The two key questions: Are the penalties reasonable? And, do you have money elsewhere for emergencies? If so, when an emergency arises, go to your money market account and get some money there. If you need more money, go to your passbook savings. Need more money? Go to the interest in your CD.

Grandfathered means products purchased before the effective date of the tax change remain to be taxed more favorably.

22. Your spouse and children could spend 100% of the death benefit in the first year, but you can do something about that.

Annuity owners control when they pay income taxes on their tax-deferred earnings. They simply surrender, withdraw, or annuitize. They also control who gets their money after they die and how they can get it. If you feel that it is in the best interest of your beneficiary(ies) to get your money on a monthly or quarterly basis over 5 years or over their lifetime, instead of a single lump sum, you can request a restricted beneficiary form from the insurer or you can add your request on the application. As always, consult your legal advisors and have a talk with your loved ones.

23. The issue date of your annuity might help your beneficiaries legally avoid paying income taxes on all of the tax-deferred interest.

At your death, your spouse, if named the beneficiary on your non-qualified annuity contract, can continue your annuity and enjoy tax deferral indefinitely or she can surrender and pay income taxes on the tax-deferred earnings. However, if you purchased an Investment Annuity before March 7, 1977, or a Variable Annuity before October 21, 1979, ask your tax advisor if you still have the "Stepped-Up Cost basis provision" that may have been preserved when taxation changed. If so, the cost basis of the annuity would move up to the annuity value on the day annuity owner died. As a result, the beneficiary can get all of the tax-deferred earnings with no income taxes due at all.

24. Ninety-three% of annuity owners still own the first annuity that they purchased.[1]

93% of annuity owners surveyed reported that they still owned the first annuity that they purchased. While 86% of the owners purchased their first annuity before age 65, the average annuity owner is now age 70. Regarding education, 53% of annuity owners have graduated from college and 26% have completed, at least, some post graduate work. Possible lesson to be learned? There are a lot of smart people who are happy with the annuity decision they first made.

25. I need the same thing that you do.

I do not mind if Mrs. Harris works. I do mind if Mrs. Harris has to work. There is a big difference between the two. I never want to ask my two sons, Will and Chris, for a loan. I never want my daughter, Elizabeth, to give me a bath. I need the same thing that you want and need, financial and emotional independence. Reading this book, consulting with your tax and legal advisors, thinking about your money regularly, and reaching out to your bank, insurance, and investment professionals are examples of you being the best that you can be for your spouse, children, and grandchildren.

---

[1]*Source: NAVA 2008 Annuity Fact Book. The Committee of Annuity Insurers commissioned Gallup surveys nine times since 1992. These surveys were developed by the Committee of Annuity Insurers, The Gallup Organization, and Mathew Greenwald & Associates and they asked owners of non-qualified annuities for data and opinions. The facts cited above were from that survey.*

26. There might be an easier way to wait until age 70 in order to get enhanced retirement benefits from Social Security.

As the hypothetical chart on page 47 illustrated, waiting to receive Social Security benefits until age 70 instead of beginning payments at age 62 resulted in cumulative payments of $332,000 compared to cumulative payments of $261,000 by starting Social Security at age 62. Naturally, the difference between cumulative payments with an age 62 start date versus an age 70 start date would have been less if one died before age 90 and more if they lived beyond age 90. (please look at the chart on page 47)

However, we now open the door to alternative ways in which one can wait until age 70. Obviously working part time and/or spending less could help you forgo a $750 a month lifetime Social Security benefit beginning at age 62 in anticipation of a much richer $1,340 lifetime Social Security benefit beginning at age 70 would be one alternative.

Two More Alternatives

Those individuals or couples approaching the age of 62 who have money outside of Qualified Plans have two extra alternatives.

1. Bank Saving Accounts

You can ask your bank to withdraw $750 from your savings account each month and redeposit that $750 into your checking account each month for eight years from age 62 to age 70, the age the enhanced Social Security benefits begin. This way, you can delay receiving Social Security but still get the $750. The cost of this would be depleting a savings account but the cumulative potential higher Social Security benefits could offset this cost in whole or in part depending upon when death occurs. See the examples on the next page.

2. Period Certain Immediate Annuities

One of the two best kept secrets in the financial industry is that insurance companies can offer guaranteed income for 5, 6, 7, 8, 9, and 10 years with NO life contingency. For example, the insurer can guarantee monthly payments for 8 years. If you die after one year, your beneficiaries are guaranteed to receive $750 a month for 7 more years. At the end of the 8th year, monthly payments stop regardless to whether you are alive or not. It is called a Period Certain Immediate Annuity.

This way, you can delay receiving Social Security until age 70 but still get the $750 a month but from the 8 Year Term and Period Certain Immediate Annuity, not Social Security. The cost of this would be the single premium you make to the insurer for the 8 Year Term and Period Certain Immediate Annuity. However, the cumulative potential higher Social Security benefits could offset this cost in whole or in part depending upon when death occurs during the time you are receiving Social Security. See the examples on the next page.

The Second Best Kept Secret About Immediate Annuities

Firstly, the difference between what one insurance company guarantees each month and what another insurance company can guarantee can vary a great deal. In other words, shop for the lowest possible premium in order to get, for example, $750 a month guaranteed for 8 years. But remember, the guarantees that an insurance company makes are only as strong as the insurance company making the guarantees. Fortunately, some of the most respected insurance companies now offer Period Certain Immediate Annuities.

Secondly, there are times during the year, when a handful of insurers really lower the cost to getting an Immediate Annuity. Again, shop.

Without really shopping for the most competitive Bank product and 8 Year Period Certain Immediate Annuity, we have illustrated some examples to what one could expect to pay for a payment of $750 a month for 8 years. In other words, try to beat these, then consult with your advisors for their opinion. Why? Circumstances differ from one individual to another individual and what is best for one is not necessarily best for another individual.

Bank Products:
$69,000 in the bank earning 1.00 % could generate $750 a month for 8 years with taxable interest of $2,818 over those 8 years.

$70,500 in the bank earning .50 % could generate $750 a month for 8 years with taxable interest of $1,433 over those 8 years.

$71,250 in the bank earning .25% could generate $750 a month for 8 years with taxable interest of $722.00 over those 8 years.

Disadvantages:
1) Almost all Bank CDs will have substantial withdrawal

Continued Bank Product: Disadvantages)

penalties for pre-mature withdrawals; and a withdrawal of $750 a month will most likely impose a penalty. As a result, your Bank product will most apt be a Passbook Savings or Money Market account, not a higher interest CD earning 1%.

2) Since interest rates are not guaranteed for a long period of time, interest rates could go lower (but not much lower since rates are already real low); meaning that your account could deplete to zero before $750 a month could be paid for 8 years if Bank interest rates decrease.

Advantages:
If interest rates were to increase, you are more apt to receive a higher interest rate; meaning you could have some money remaining in your account after receiving $750 a month for 8 years.

8 Year Period Certain Immediate Annuity
Insurance Company A $ 67,518 will generate $750 a month for 8 years; 94 % income tax free.

Insurance Company B $ 68,502 will generate $750 a month for 8 years; 95%% income tax free.

Insurance Company C $ 71,306 will generate $750 a month for 8 years; 99% income tax free.

Disadvantages:
1) If interest rates increase (or decrease), your payments will not change.

2) Your annuity will not be FDIC insured but it will be backed by the claims-paying ability of the insurance company issuing the Immediate Annuity.

Advantages:
1) Potentially lower cost since a $67,518 premium is less than the $69,000-$71,000 you would need at a bank.

2) A substantial portion of the payments received will be excludable from income taxes since they are considered a return of premium.

3) Your $750.00 a month payments are guaranteed for 8 years; no more and no less than 8 years.

27. Recovering losses is far more difficult than losing the money.

Losses during the 2008-2009 market downturn is one of the reasons why so many have not retired yet. However, with the stock market recovery, one would think that most investors who stayed invested from 2008-2009 until January 2013 have now recovered all or almost all their losses and can now retire.

Sadly, recovering losses is far more difficult than "just" losing some of your money. For example, many investors saw their retirement nest egg plummet 35% in 2008-2009, in other words, every $100,000 invested became worth $65,000.

So it made a great deal of sense to far too many that all they needed was a 35% gain to recover their 35% loss. And when that occurred, they could retire.

Neil Sedaka sang in 1962 "Breaking up is hard to do." We are reporting in 2013, that "Recovering losses is even harder to do."

With $100,000 decreasing 35% to $65,000; you would need a gain of 54% for $65,000 to return to $100,000.

With $100,000 decreasing 45% to $55,000; you would need a gain of 81 % for $55,000 to return to $100,000.

With $100,000 decreasing 55% to $45,000; you would need a gain of 122 % for $45,000 to return to $100,000.

Lessons learned:
• Recovering losses is a lot harder than losing money.

• Be more conservative when within 5 -10 years of retiring.

• Consider products where double digit losses are impossible; certainly when nearing retirement or during retirement.

• Diversify

28. 65 year old plus workers increase by almost 60%

The Bureau of Labor Statistics reports that the number of Americans working after age 65 has increased by almost 60% in the last decade. W.V.H.,Inc. reports that all of the following factors contributed to the substantial increase of 65 year old plus workers still busy at work: 1) enhanced Social Security benefits if retirement begins at age 70, 2) historically all time low interest rates at banks, 3) savers and investors still hoping to recoup 100% of 2008-2009 losses, and the "Aging and Education of America."

29. The "Aging and Education of America."

On pages 37-41, we unveil almost hard to believe statistics from experts about longer live expectancy. Unquestionably, these statistics and just watching people live and live have convinced even the skeptics that they and their loved ones are more likely to live longer than they had thought.

However, it will be "The Education Of America" that will give "More Life" to those added years. This book is one example to how people can add " more life" to their years by lessening the impact of inflation, relying less on Social Security, paying income taxes later instead of now, potentially accumulating more money, and the financial dignity of electing lifetime income.

When you read books like ours about "financial health" plus other types of books about "medical health" and when you attend webinars and seminars about both types of health— financial and medical—you are fulfilling your responsibilities as spouse, parent, and grandparent; not to mention affecting how your loved ones will remember you.

30. 1982 What a year to retire!

One could say that 1982 was a much better time to retire than today. In 1982, Bank CDs & Tax Deferred Annuities were paying 15% interest. So every $100,000 in the bank or annuity could generate $15,000 of annual income. In other words, $500,000 of savings could trigger income of $75,000 a year....and a lot could be purchased for that $75,000 since a brand new Cadillac Coupe Deville was only $15,000 and a very nice home was $52,000.

In 2012, only 30 years later, $500,000 spread out among 2 or more banks would generate annual income of $5,000 or less a year........instead of the $75,000 a year that "lucky" 1982 retirees received.

Or are we really the lucky ones? While current interest rates are low, recent innovative product designs in the insurance industry such as lifetime income riders, new ways to save more money via 401(k)s, employer matching, catch-up provisions, and a re-birth of older products made better are ironically making some Americans financially and emotionally independent.

(smile) While it is too late for you to retire in 1982, it may not be too late for you to be among that group of "some Americans" who retire with dignity. Would you like to retire with dignity?

Product Descriptions

Since *75 Secrets* addresses Certificates of Deposit (CDs), and Tax-Deferred Annuities, and the importance of retirement planning, the following pages dive deeper into CDs and annuities. Hopefully, you will see that both CDs and annuities deserve your attention for some of your money. Neither CDs nor annuities deserve to get all of your money since you should never put all of your money in any one product. However, you, your tax and legal advisors, and then your insurance professional are more qualified than we to know what is in your best interest. Just turn the page to become more informed.

What is a Certificate of Deposit?

A Certificate of Deposit—often referred to as a CD—is a special type of deposit account with a bank or thrift institution that typically offers a higher rate of interest than a regular savings account. Unlike other investments, CDs feature federal deposit insurance (FDIC).

Here's how CDs work: When you purchase a CD, you invest a fixed sum of money for a fixed period of time like six months, one year, five years, or more—and, in exchange, the issuing bank pays you interest, typically at regular intervals. When you cash in or redeem your CD, you receive the money you originally invested plus any accrued interest. However, if you redeem your CD before it matures, you may have to pay an "early withdrawal" penalty or forfeit a portion of the interest you earned.

Although most savers purchase CDs through local banks, many brokerage firms now offer CDs. These brokerage firms—known as "deposit brokers" — can sometimes negotiate a higher rate of interest for a CD by promising to bring a certain amount of deposits to the institution. The deposit broker can then offer these "brokered CDs" to their customers.

At one time, most CDs paid a fixed interest rate until they reached maturity. But, like many other products in today's markets, CDs have become more complicated. Investors may now choose among variable rate CDs, long-term CDs, and CDs with special redemption features in the event the owner dies.

Some long-term, high-yield CDs have "call" features, meaning that the issuing bank may choose to terminate—or call—the CD before maturity. Only the issuing bank may call a CD, not the investor. For example, a bank might decide to call its high-yield CDs if interest rates fall. However, if you've invested in a long-term CD and interest rates subsequently rise, you'll be locked in at the lower rate.

Before you consider purchasing a CD from your bank or brokerage firm, make sure you fully understand all of its terms. Carefully read the disclosure statements, including any fine print. Don't be dazzled by high yields, and ask questions and demand answers before you invest.

Almost all of the above came from: http://www.fdic.gov/deposit/deposits/certificate.

What are Annuities?

Annuities are insurance products offered by insurance companies. There are 2 categories of annuities: Immediate Annuities and Tax-Deferred Annuities. Immediate Annuities provide guaranteed income either for life or for a period of years. On the other hand, Tax -Deferred Annuities provide tax-deferred accumulation at the onset with the option to elect guaranteed income later or continue tax-deferred accumulation.

There are four types of Tax-Deferred Annuities. Three of the four types have no market risk. The one type of annuity that has market risk offers a potentially higher return than the other three types of annuities that have no market risk. All 4 types of annuities have surrender charges for a period of time that could result in a loss of premium if surrendered prematurely.

Each of the 4 types of annuities credit interest and earnings differently.

Variable

1. Variable Annuity: Since you can select among a wide variety of professionally managed investment options with varying risk and reward potential, earnings, if any, are credited based upon performance and accumulate tax-deferred.

    - market risk: yes
    - annual fees and expenses: yes
    - riders: yes, a wide variety of living and death benefit riders
    - surrender charges: yes

Fixed Annuities

2. Indexed Annuities: The insurer credits interest based on a percentage of the increases, if any, in an external index such as The Dow Jones Industrial Average^{SM}; there are many different ways insurers can credit interest such as Annual Reset, High Water, Point to Point, etc. For example, with Annual Reset, when the index decreases during the contract year, 0% interest can be credited. When the index increases during the contract year, you can get, for example, 50% of the increases in the index. Arguably, this is a nice compromise for those who have a low tolerance for risk but who still seek interest potentially higher than the other two types of Fixed Annuities and Certificates of Deposit.

Fixed Annuities/Indexed Annuities (continued)
- market risk: no
- annual fees and expenses: yes, with some Indexed Annuities
- riders: yes, Lifetime Income rider with some Indexed Annuities is available along with other riders
- surrender charges: yes
- market value adjustment: possible

3. Multi-Year Guarantee Annuities: The insurer guarantees to credit a specified interest rate for 1-10 years; often the interest rate guarantee period matches the duration of the surrender charge period; Multi-Year Guarantee Annuities guaranteeing higher interest rates often have a Market Value Adjustment.

- market risk: no
- annual fees and expenses: only a handful
- riders: yes
- surrender charges: yes
- market value adjustment: very possible in order for interest rates to be more competitive

4. Traditional Annuities: Normally the interest rate is for one year and sometimes includes a bonus interest rate; at the end of each year, the insurer declares a new interest rate for the following year; typically surrender charges do not disappear at the end of each year.

- market risk: no
- annual fees and expenses: only a handful
- riders: yes
- surrender charges: yes
- market value adjustment: possible

Summary

Almost all of the 4 types of annuities offer tax-deferred accumulation, potential probate advantages, liquidity via a 10% free partial withdrawal, the option to elect guaranteed monthly income via annuitization, and surrender charges. While Indexed Annuities, Multi-Year Guarantee Annuities, and Traditional Annuities offer a guaranteed minimum interest rate for the life of the policy, Variable Annuities do not.

Overly simplified, with the Variable Annuity, the risk is assumed by the annuity owner and the return could be potentially higher than Fixed Annuities. With the 3 Fixed Annuities, risk is assumed by the insurer since the insurer is guaranteeing a guaranteed minimum value each year, a lifetime interest rate for the life of the policy, and a guaranteed selling price* since you will also know the surrender charges for each year and when they disappear.

*Assuming an annuity with no market value adjustment.

Next Steps
- Consult with your tax and legal advisors regarding CDs and annuities.
- Reach out to your banker, insurance professional and investment professional for their recommendations.
- Circle back to your tax and legal advisors regarding the products that you are considering.
- Diversify; never put all of your eggs in one basket.
- Understand what you are buying.
- Take cautious baby steps.
- Read and understand what you are signing.

Advantages and Disadvantages

E very decision you make in your day-to-day personal life has advantages and disadvantages. And, selecting a retirement product is no different. All you have to do is to weigh the advantages and disadvantages in order to see what is in your best interest. Fortunately, with a retirement product, there are "steps" that you can take that will increase the probability of you making a wise decision. Those "steps" appeared on the last page of almost every secret.

On the following pages, we list the advantages and disadvantages of owning Certificates of Deposit and Tax- Deferred Annuities. Please show these to your tax and legal advisors, banker, and to your insurance and/or investment professional so they can either offer you more advantages and disadvantages, elaborate on ours, or disagree. They know you and their products better than we.

Advantages of Certificates of Deposit (CDs)

Safe
CDs at FDIC insured banks can be insured up to $250,000. Coverage is scheduled to decrease to $100,000 for most accounts on January 1, 2014.

Liquid
The bank pays you interest at regular intervals. When you cash in your CD at maturity, you receive your principal plus any accrued interest.

Interest Rates
During an increasing and decreasing interest rate environment, historically, banks have been able to react to current interest rates quickly and can potentially offer higher and lower interest rates for new CD purchases. Shopping for the highest interest rate is also easy since online services and newspapers identify the banks paying the highest rates daily. While CDs bought from a broker can be different than a CD bought from the bank, a "Brokered" CD often pays a higher interest since the "brokerage firm" has negotiated a higher rate for its clients.

Death Benefit
Some CDs offer a death benefit that allows the beneficiary to redeem the CD without penalty if the CD owner were to die.

Disadvantages of Certificates of Deposit (CDs)

Maturity

Since FDIC coverage is scheduled to decrease to $100,000 for most accounts except some retirement accounts like IRAs on January 1, 2014, one should make sure that they do not have a maturity date after January 1, 2014 if principal and accrued interest might exceed $100,000.

Taxation

Like most taxable products, interest is taxable even when interest is not withdrawn.

Callable CDs

Some long-term CDs have "call" features so the bank can terminate the CD after some fixed period of time, for example, if interest rates fall. If this would occur, you could get your initial principal plus any accrued interest without penalty. So if you own a callable long-term CD, you might not be locking in an interest rate since the bank can terminate and offer you a lower interest rate. On the other hand, if you've invested in a long-term CD and interest rates subsequently rise, you'll be locked in at the lower rate since the bank will most likely not "call" your CD.

The Issuer

According to the FDIC, "because federal deposit insurance is limited in each bank or thrift institution, it is very important that you know which bank or thrift issued your CD". In other words, find out where the deposit broker plans to deposit your money. Also be sure to ask what record-keeping procedures the deposit broker has in place to assure your CD will have federal deposit insurance. For more information about federal deposit protection insurance, read the FDIC's publication *Your Insured Deposits* or call the FDIC's Central Call Center at (877) 275-3342 or (877) ASK-FDIC."

(Continued on next page)

Certificates of Deposit

(Disadvantages continued)

Penalties

Understandably, there is a premature withdrawal penalty if the CD is redeemed prior to maturity. Penalties can range from 30 days' loss of interest for a 30 day CD to one year's loss of interest for CD maturities exceeding 36 months. Surprising to some, penalties can result in you getting back less than your initial principal if you were to redeem your CD too early before sufficient interest was earned.

According to the FDIC, "Research any penalties for early withdrawal. Be sure to find out how much you'll have to pay if you cash in your CD before maturity. For example, some brokered CDs are issued in the name of the "custodian" or deposit broker. In some cases, the deposit broker may advertise that the CD does not have a prepayment penalty for early withdrawal. In those cases, the deposit broker will instead try to resell the CD for you if you want to redeem it before maturity. If interest rates have fallen since you purchased your CD and demand is high, you may be able to sell the CD for a profit. But if interest rates have risen, there may be less demand for your lower-yielding CD. That means you may have to sell the CD at a discount and lose some of your original deposit."

Advantages of Annuities

Time
The more time you have before retiring or the more time you have before needing income during retirement, the more powerful tax deferral becomes. As you saw in some of the Secrets, time can be a friend or an enemy. Understandably, the younger you are, the less apt you are to have a lot of money to put into a tax-deferred annuity. Therefore, there are some annuities that can allow you to start by making flexible premiums every month or every quarter.

Reducing Or Eliminating Taxes On Social Security Income
Repositioning some of your money that you have in taxable alternatives to a tax-deferred annuity may reduce or eliminate the income taxes that you are paying on your Social Security benefits. Please see Secret 53.

Guaranteed Income
Many retirees are on a fixed income and are living far longer than expected. As a result, too many are outliving their money. The annuity is the only product that can guarantee monthly income for as long as you and/or your spouse are alive with part of the payments excluded from income taxes. Simply put, an annuity owner can either purchase an immediate annuity with a single premium or they can apply the values built up in their tax-deferred annuity and annuitize their annuity to receive income that they cannot outlive. Please see Secret 57 plus the end of this section where Immediate Annuities are discussed.

Tax-Deferred Accumulation
Under current tax law, earnings credited to annuities accumulate tax deferred until withdrawn. This can be an advantage for those who do not need income yet. As you are aware, earnings credited to taxable alternatives are taxable even if not withdrawn.

(Continued on next page)

(Advantages of Annuities continued)

Partial Access To Your Money in Early Years

In many tax-deferred annuity contracts, owners may withdraw a percentage of their dollars free of surrender charges. With many annuity contracts, the penalty free withdrawal percentage is often 10% of the accumulation value with penalty-free withdrawals allowed beginning in the 2nd contract year. This provision can vary from one annuity contract to another and pre-tax withdrawals prior to age 59.5 may be subject to 10% federal tax penalty in addition to regular income taxes. Naturally, the advantage of penalty-free partial access surfaces if the owner needs money unexpectedly and the money needed exceeds the emergency funds they have outside the annuity.

Total Access To Your Money in Later Years

In some annuity contracts, the surrender charges permanently disappear to 0% after the surrender charge period. In other annuity contracts, surrender charges disappear after the surrender charge period, but the surrender charges can reappear after a 30 day window like if the owner chooses to renew for another period of time. In both instances, the annuity owner may surrender or exchange their annuity without any surrender charges assuming they surrender when there are no surrender charges. Naturally, a surrender would be a taxable event, but the surrender could be carefully timed when in a lower tax bracket. A 1035(a) exchange from one annuity to another annuity is income tax-free and could be beneficial if the new annuity is appreciably superior to the older annuity. And, the new annuity should be appreciably better than the older annuity since the new annuity will have a new surrender charge period.

Potentially More Money Later

As discussed earlier, annuity owners could have more money later since earnings accumulate 3 different ways: earnings compound on top of premium, earnings compound of top of earnings, and earnings can compound on top of the dollars that normally go to the government in income taxes.

(Advantages of Annuities continued on next page)

(Advantages of Annuities continued)

Less Current Income Taxes Now

Taxes are only paid when earnings are withdrawn from the annuity in comparison to interest earned on taxable alternatives when taxes are paid regardless of whether you leave the interest in or take the interest out. Naturally, these dollars that you would normally pay in taxes now remain in the annuity to help accumulate more money. Just as the annuity is the only financial product that can guarantee income for life, the Fixed Annuity is the only financial product that can guarantee an interest rate for the life of the policy.

Probate Advantages

Clearly, one of the most overlooked benefits to owning an annuity is that dollars paid to a named beneficiary can avoid the delay, expense, and publicity of probate. This annuity advantage could potentially mean thousands of extra dollars and potentially less anxiety for the beneficiaries.

Another Way To Diversify

In the opinion of many, no one should put a great deal of their dollars into any one given concept and/or product. People should carefully diversify their dollars among taxable, tax-deferred and tax-free alternatives. As a result, annuities become an excellent candidate for "some" of your dollars so that you can diversify more thoroughly.

Wide Variety of Riders

Annuities can provide both riders and surrender charge waivers for various crises like nursing home confinement, terminal illness, etc.. These riders can provide liquidity, guarantees, and flexibility. However, you should fully understand how they work and what they cost so you can determine their value.

Surrender Charges

While some view surrender charges as a disadvantage, others view surrender charges as a plus since a) the surrender penalty is known up front, and b) they do protect an insurer from a "run on the bank." Please see Secrets 59, 61, and 67.

Multi-Year Interest Rate Guarantees

Since some annuities offer interest rate guarantees for 1-10 years, you can ladder a series of different annuities or a series of different interest rate guarantee periods inside of one annuity and protect yourself to some extent from interest rate uncertainty. Please see Secret 75.

(Continued on next page)

(Advantages of Annuities continued)

Follow respected indexes (Indexed Annuities only)

Some annuities credit interest based on a percent of the increases in an index like the Dow Jones Industrial Average[SM] and credit 0% when the index decreases. Please see Secret 71 for the rest of the story.

Professional Management (Variable Annuities only)

Variable Annuities allow you to select a wide variety of sub accounts managed by professionals so that your money potentially grows faster than Fixed Annuities.

Disadvantages of Annuities

Surrender Charges

Generally speaking, a consumer age 60 and older is more apt to need access to their tax-deferred earnings earlier than a younger consumer since they are more apt to be retired and/or more apt to have special medical needs for themselves or for their spouse. Therefore, liquidity is more important. While the existence of surrender charges in most annuity contracts makes sense, consumers age 60 and older should lean to annuities with a shorter surrender charge period and smaller surrender penalties. Regardless of a short or long surrender charge period, you should have at least 6 months' income set aside for emergencies, an understanding to when you might need retirement income to begin, and money outside the annuity in case retirement income is needed earlier.

Taxation

Since tax-deferral has been awarded to annuities as a retirement vehicle, there are tax penalties if an owner withdraws or surrenders prior to age 59½. To be more exact, there is a 10% tax penalty for pre-tax dollars withdrawn before age 59½. Therefore, people younger than age 59½ should not turn to the Annuity for partial or total access to their dollars. Hopefully, they will turn to dollars that they have wisely placed in other alternatives.

Death Benefit

Unfortunately, a consumer age 60 and older is more apt to die than a consumer many years younger. Some annuities subject the death benefit to a surrender charge; others do not. In addition, some annuities pay the death benefit to the beneficiary if the owner dies; others pay the death benefit to the beneficiary if the annuitant dies; this only becomes a major disadvantage if you have not designated the correct party as beneficiary. Please see Secret 62 to learn how to easily correct the situation.

(Continued on next page)

(Disadvantages of Annuities continued)

Increasing Interest Rates (Traditional Fixed Annuities)

In an increasing interest rate environment, interest rates that many traditional Fixed Annuities pay in renewal years do not tend to increase as rapidly as the market. This potentially could affect those on a fixed income during an increasing interest rate environment. One solution is to diversify more so that the money you have in the bank can react to increasing interest rates and the annuity could help you in a decreasing or level interest rate environment. Naturally, another solution to potential increasing interest rates or decreasing interest rates for that matter would be Laddering annuities.

Renewal Rates (Fixed Annuities only)

Some insurers have not paid competitive renewal interest rates. Since initial current interest rates are not guaranteed forever, you might want to review the history of renewal interest rates for both the product and insurer you are considering. Or, select an annuity with a Multi-Year Interest Rate Guarantee and a surrender charge period that lasts as long as the interest rate guarantee.

Strength of Insurer

Since an insurance company's guarantees are only as strong as the insurer issuing the annuity, you can evaluate an insurer by reading what the independent rating services are saying about the insurer. Since independent rating services are not always right, your advisors can examine how the insurer invests their assets and the insurer's capital and surplus. Regardless, it almost always makes good business sense to diversify your dollars among different insurers, banks for dollars exceeding FDIC limits, and money market funds.

Fees

We add fees as a disadvantage only because fees are perceived too often as always a disadvantage by some. In actuality, you are paying a fee in order to get something in return. Every morning, I pay Starbucks a fee. In return, I get coffee. To be fair, we would wholeheartedly agree that fees become a disadvantage if they are excessive or if the fees offer you a value far less than you expected or far less than you now want. To summarize, a few Traditional Annuities and annuities with a Multi-Year Interest Rate Guarantee have fees; some Indexed Annuities have fees; and, understandably, all Variable Annuities have fees. Regarding the Lifetime Income Riders that both Fixed and Variable Annuities have, there are either fees or the fees are built into the pricing of the annuity. As your Mom and Dad probably told you, "There is no such thing as a free lunch." And, they were right again.

(Continued on next page)

(Disadvantages of Annuities continued)

Market Value Adjustment

Some Fixed Annuities have a Market Value Adjustment. While a Market Value Adjustment protects your annuity carrier from a run on the bank during a time when interest rates are rising, a Market Value Adjustment (MVA) is another type of penalty if you withdraw too much or surrender during the Market Value Adjustment period. Generally speaking, annuity owners who have incurred a negative Market Value Adjustment in the past are those who:

1. have placed too much of their money into an annuity at the onset
2. did not have 6 months' of income outside the annuity in highly liquid FDIC insured accounts
3. sadly, had a devastating event
4. were too easily convinced to make a surrender
5. made the wrong decision
6. did not reach out to their tax or legal advisor before purchase

Fortunately, you can control 5 of those 6 things so a negative Market Value Adjustment and/or Surrender Charges never take a bite out of your retirement money.

Immediate Annuities

The backbone of every tax-deferred annuity is that you can elect, if you wish, guaranteed income for as long as you live or for as long as you or your spouse are alive. Or, you can even elect guaranteed income for a set period of time from 5 to 30 years where payments can be paid to you while you are alive and then to your beneficiaries for the balance of the time period that you selected. For examples of the 7 ways to receive income, please see Secret 60. This is called annuitization and it is very different from receiving income from some of the Lifetime Income Riders discussed in Secret 64 and 68.

Advantages of Immediate Annuities

The Advantages to Annuitizing A Tax-Deferred Annuity Later Or Purchasing An Immediate Annuity At The Onset

- Less anxiety. You are assured of a guaranteed stream of income for x years or for as long as you and/or your spouse are alive.
- You will not outlive your money.
- Tax-advantaged income. Since an exclusion ratio is used to determine the percentage of dollars excludable from income taxes, only part of the income you receive during your life expectancy from a non-qualified annuity will be taxable. (The income excluded from income taxes is considered a return of your premium.)
- Some states protect Immediate Annuities, to some extent, from creditors. See Secret 54.

Disadvantages of Immediate Annuities

The Disadvantages to Annuitizing A Tax-Deferred Annuity Later Or Purchasing An Immediate Annuity At The Onset

- You cannot, generally speaking, surrender your Immediate Annuity and reinvest those proceeds in another alternative.
- In an increasing interest rate environment, your fixed payments from your Fixed Annuity will remain fixed in spite of higher interest rates.

As you can see, the annuity has advantages and disadvantages. Fortunately, the advantages can be quite impressive. But, just like every product, there are disadvantages. You and your tax and legal advisors should weigh and balance the disadvantages based upon your time horizon, tolerance for risk, wants and needs, the amount of money you have set aside for emergencies, and the amount of money you have in other annuities.

10 Special Visuals

This section contains a library of helpful tables, memorable charts, and tax-reducing questionnaires. You will find yourself referring to this section often since the questionnaires can potentially help you, your parents, or grandparents reduce taxes, the tables will help you fight the impact of inflation, and the charts allow you to walk down memory lane and reflect on your life. Said differently, this section has research that took W.V.H. Inc., years to compile. Just turn the page to find your new library of 10 special visuals.

The next 10 visuals

Eroding Purchasing Power of $10,000						
	Inflation					
Year	1%	2%	3%	4%	5%	6%
1	$9,900	$9,800	$9,700	$9,600	$9,500	$9,400
2	$9,801	$9,604	$9,409	$9,216	$9,025	$8,836
3	$9,703	$9,412	$9,127	$8,847	$8,574	$8,306
4	$9,606	$9,224	$8,853	$8,493	$8,145	$7,807
5	$9,510	$9,039	$8,587	$8,154	$7,738	$7,339
6	$9,415	$8,858	$8,330	$7,828	$7,351	$6,899
7	$9,321	$8,681	$8,080	$7,514	$6,983	$6,485
8	$9,227	$8,508	$7,837	$7,214	$6,634	$6,096
9	$9,135	$8,337	$7,602	$6,925	$6,302	$5,730
10	$9,044	$8,171	$7,374	$6,648	$5,987	$5,386
11	$8,953	$8,007	$7,153	$6,382	$5,688	$5,063
12	$8,864	$7,847	$6,938	$6,127	$5,404	$4,759
13	$8,775	$7,690	$6,730	$5,882	$5,133	$4,474
14	$8,687	$7,536	$6,528	$5,647	$4,877	$4,205
15	$8,601	$7,386	$6,333	$5,421	$4,633	$3,953
16	$8,515	$7,238	$6,143	$5,204	$4,401	$3,716
17	$8,429	$7,093	$5,958	$4,996	$4,181	$3,493
18	$8,345	$6,951	$5,780	$4,796	$3,972	$3,283
19	$8,262	$6,812	$5,606	$4,604	$3,774	$3,086
20	$8,179	$6,676	$5,438	$4,420	$3,585	$2,901
21	$8,097	$6,543	$5,275	$4,243	$3,406	$2,727
22	$8,016	$6,412	$5,117	$4,073	$3,235	$2,563
23	$7,936	$6,283	$4,963	$3,911	$3,074	$2,410
24	$7,857	$6,158	$4,814	$3,754	$2,920	$2,265
25	$7,778	$6,035	$4,670	$3,604	$2,774	$2,129
26	$7,700	$5,914	$4,530	$3,460	$2,635	$2,001
27	$7,623	$5,796	$4,394	$3,321	$2,503	$1,881
28	$7,547	$5,680	$4,262	$3,189	$2,378	$1,768
29	$7,472	$5,566	$4,134	$3,061	$2,259	$1,662
30	$7,397	$5,455	$4,010	$2,939	$2,146	$1,563

Social Security worksheet for your tax advisor to review.

| Worksheet A. | **A Quick Way To Check if Your Benefits May Be Taxable** | *Keep for your records* |

A.   Enter the amount from **box 5** of all your Forms SSA-1099 and RRB-1099. Include the full amount of any lump-sum benefit payments received in 2012, for 2012 and earlier years. (If you received more than one form, combine the amounts from box 5 and enter the total.) . . . . A. _____

Note. If the amount on line A is zero or less, stop here; none of your benefits are taxable this year.

B.   Enter one-half of the amount on line A . . . . B. _____

C.   Enter your taxable pensions, wages, interest, dividends, and other taxable income . . . . C. _____

D.   Enter any tax-exempt interest income (such as interest on municipal bonds) plus any exclusions from income (listed earlier) . . . . D. _____

E.   Add lines B, C, and D . . . . E. _____

Note. Compare the amount on line E to your **base amount** for your filing status. If the amount on line E equals or is less than the **base amount** for your filing status, none of your benefits are taxable this year. If the amount on line E is more than your **base amount,** some of your benefits may be taxable. You need to complete Worksheet 1, shown later. If none of your benefits are taxable, but you otherwise must file a tax return, see *Benefits not taxable,* later, under *How To Report Your Benefits.*

| Worksheet A. | **A Quick Way To Check if Your Benefits May Be Taxable** | *Keep for your records* |

A.   Enter the amount from **box 5** of all your Forms SSA-1099 and RRB-1099. Include the full amount of any lump-sum benefit payments received in 2012, for 2012 and earlier years. (If you received more than one form, combine the amounts from box 5 and enter the total.) . . . . A. $12,000

Note. If the amount on line A is zero or less, stop here; none of your benefits are taxable this year.

B.   Enter one-half of the amount on line A . . . . B. $6,000

C.   Enter your taxable pensions, wages, interest, dividends, and other taxable income . . . . C. $34,000

D.   Enter any tax-exempt interest income (such as interest on municipal bonds) plus any exclusions from income (listed earlier) . . . . D. $800

E.   Add lines B, C, and D . . . . E. $40,800

Note. Compare the amount on line E to your **base amount** for your filing status. If the amount on line E equals or is less than the **base amount** for your filing status, none of your benefits are taxable this year. If the amount on line E is more than your **base amount,** some of your benefits may be taxable. You need to complete Worksheet 1, shown later. If none of your benefits are taxable, but you otherwise must file a tax return, see *Benefits not taxable,* later, under *How To Report Your Benefits.*

If the amount on line E is more than the base amount below, your Social Security benefits may be taxable.

Your Filing Status	Base Amount
Married filing jointly	$32,000
Single	$25,000
Married filing separately	$25,000

Social Security worksheet for your tax advisor to review.

Social Security Benefits Worksheet—Lines 20a and 20b   *Keep for Your Records*

Before you begin:	✓ Complete Form 1040, lines 21 and 23 through 32, if they apply to you.
	✓ Figure any write-in adjustments to be entered on the dotted line next to line 36 (see the instructions for line 36).
	✓ If you are married filing separately and you lived apart from your spouse for all of 2013, enter "D" to the right of the word "benefits" on line 20a. If you do not, you may get a math error notice from the IRS.
	✓ Be sure you have read the **Exception** in the line 20a and 20b instructions to see if you can use this worksheet instead of a publication to find out if any of your benefits are taxable.

1. Enter the total amount from **box 5** of **all** your **Forms SSA-1099** and **Forms RRB-1099.** Also, enter this amount on Form 1040, line 20a .... **1.** _____

2. Enter one-half of line 1 .... **2.** _____

3. Combine the amounts from Form 1040, lines 7, 8a, 9a, 10 through 14, 15b, 16b, 17 through 19, and 21 .... **3.** _____

4. Enter the amount, if any, from Form 1040, line 8b .... **4.** _____

5. Combine lines 2, 3, and 4 .... **5.** _____

6. Enter the total of the amounts from Form 1040, lines 23 through 32, plus any write-in adjustments you entered on the dotted line next to line 36 .... **6.** _____

7. Is the amount on line 6 less than the amount on line 5?

   ☐ **No.** (STOP) None of your social security benefits are taxable. Enter -0- on Form 1040, line 20b.

   ☐ **Yes.** Subtract line 6 from line 5 .... **7.** _____

8. If you are:
   * Married filing jointly, enter $32,000
   * Single, head of household, qualifying widow(er), or married filing separately and you **lived apart** from your spouse for all of 2013, enter $25,000
   * Married filing separately and you lived with your spouse at any time in 2013, skip lines 8 through 15; multiply line 7 by 85% (.85) and enter the result on line 16. Then go to line 17

   .... **8.** _____

9. Is the amount on line 8 less than the amount on line 7?

   ☐ **No.** (STOP) None of your social security benefits are taxable. Enter -0- on Form 1040, line 20b. If you are married filing separately and you **lived apart** from your spouse for all of 2013, be sure you entered "D" to the right of the word "benefits" on line 20a.

   ☐ **Yes.** Subtract line 8 from line 7 .... **9.** _____

10. Enter: $12,000 if married filing jointly; $9,000 if single, head of household, qualifying widow(er), or married filing separately and you **lived apart** from your spouse for all of 2013 .... **10.** _____

11. Subtract line 10 from line 9. If zero or less, enter -0- .... **11.** _____

12. Enter the **smaller** of line 9 or line 10 .... **12.** _____

13. Enter one-half of line 12 .... **13.** _____

14. Enter the **smaller** of line 2 or line 13 .... **14.** _____

15. Multiply line 11 by 85% (.85). If line 11 is zero, enter -0- .... **15.** _____

16. Add lines 14 and 15 .... **16.** _____

17. Multiply line 1 by 85% (.85) .... **17.** _____

18. **Taxable social security benefits.** Enter the **smaller** of line 16 or line 17. Also enter this amount on Form 1040, line 20b .... **18.** _____

(TIP) *If any of your benefits are taxable for 2013 and they include a lump-sum benefit payment that was for an earlier year, you may be able to reduce the taxable amount. See Pub. 915 for details.*

All parties should consult with their own tax advisors since neither W.V.H., Inc. nor any of its employees or officers are qualified to provide tax advice.

How $100,000 accumulates tax deferred at varying interest rates.							
Year	3%	4%	5%	6%	7%	8%	9%	10%
1	$103,000	$104,000	$105,000	$106,000	$107,000	$108,000	$109,000	$110,000
2	$106,090	$108,160	$110,250	$112,360	$114,490	$116,640	$118,810	$121,000
3	$109,273	$112,486	$115,763	$119,102	$122,504	$125,971	$129,503	$133,100
4	$112,551	$116,986	$121,551	$126,248	$131,080	$136,049	$141,158	$146,410
5	$115,927	$121,665	$127,628	$133,823	$140,255	$146,933	$153,862	$161,051
10	$134,392	$148,024	$162,889	$179,085	$196,715	$215,892	$236,736	$259,374
15	$155,797	$180,094	$207,893	$239,656	$275,903	$317,217	$364,248	$417,725
20	$180,611	$219,112	$265,330	$320,714	$386,968	$466,096	$560,441	$672,750

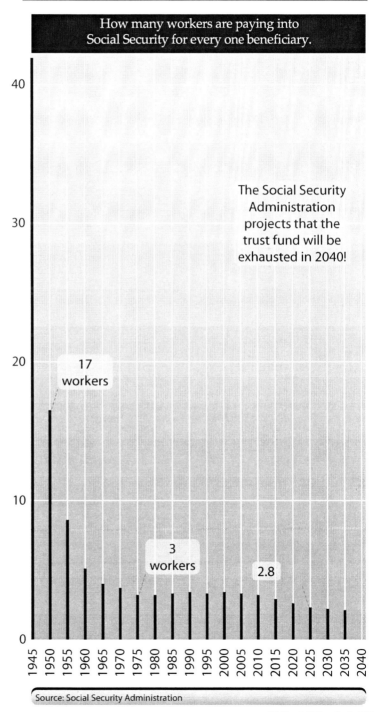

How many workers are paying into
Social Security for every one beneficiary.

The Social Security
Administration
projects that the
trust fund will be
exhausted in 2040!

17
workers

3
workers

2.8

Source: Social Security Administration

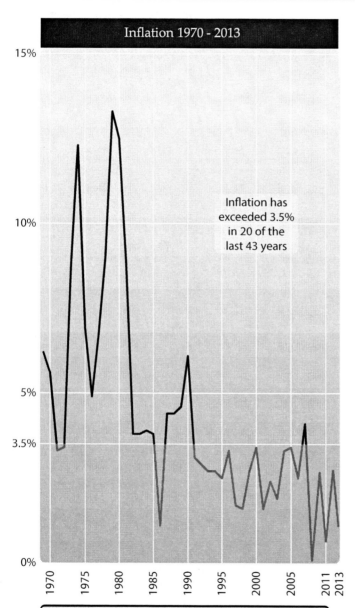

Inflation 1970 - 2013

Inflation has
exceeded 3.5%
in 20 of the
last 43 years

Since history can repeat itself, have you saved enough so
that your lifestyle will remain the same if double-digit inflation reappears? If you have not saved enough, when do
you want to begin saving more?

Source: Bureau of Labor Statistics

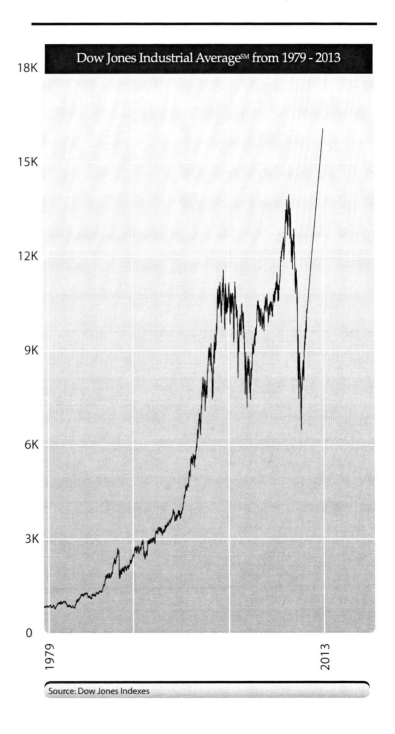

The impact that taxes and inflation can have on your return.

Year	Interest Rates*	Minimum Tax Bracket	Inflation	Real Return
1936	0.14%	4.0%	1.5%	-1.37%
1937	0.45%	4.0%	3.6%	-3.17%
1938	0.05%	4.0%	-2.1%	2.15%
1939	0.02%	4.0%	-1.4%	1.42%
1940	0.01%	4.4%	0.7%	-0.69%
1941	0.10%	10.0%	5.0%	-4.91%
1942	0.33%	19.0%	10.9%	-10.63%
1943	0.37%	19.0%	6.1%	-5.8%
1944	0.38%	23.0%	1.7%	-1.41%
1945	0.38%	23.0%	2.3%	-2.01%
1946	0.38%	19.0%	8.3%	-7.99%
1947	0.59%	19.0%	14.4%	-13.92%
1948	1.04%	16.6%	8.1%	-7.23%
1949	1.10%	16.6%	-1.2%	2.12%
1950	1.22%	17.4%	1.3%	-0.29%
1951	1.55%	20.4%	7.9%	-6.67%
1952	1.77%	22.2%	1.9%	-0.52%
1953	1.93%	22.2%	0.8%	0.70%
1954	0.95%	20.0%	0.7%	0.06%
1955	1.75%	20.0%	-0.4%	1.80%
1956	2.66%	20.0%	1.5%	0.63%
1957	3.27%	20.0%	3.3%	-0.68%
1958	1.84%	20.0%	2.8%	-1.33%
1959	3.41%	20.0%	0.7%	2.03%
1960	2.93%	20.0%	1.7%	0.64%

*Money in the bank

Sources: Bureau of Labor Statistics, United States Census Bureau, Federal Reserve Statistical Release, IRS

The impact that taxes and inflation can have on your return.				
Year	Interest Rates*	Minimum Tax Bracket	Inflation	Real Return
1961	2.38%	20.0%	1.0%	0.90%
1962	2.78%	20.0%	1.0%	1.22%
1963	3.16%	20.0%	1.3%	1.23%
1964	3.55%	16.0%	1.3%	1.68%
1965	4.76%	14.0%	1.6%	2.49%
1966	5.31%	14.0%	2.9%	1.67%
1967	4.74%	14.0%	3.1%	0.98%
1968	5.67%	14.0%	4.2%	0.68%
1969	7.12%	14.0%	5.5%	0.62%
1970	7.44%	14.0%	5.7%	0.70%
1971	4.79%	14.0%	4.4%	-0.28%
1972	4.39%	14.0%	3.2%	0.58%
1973	9.29%	14.0%	6.2%	1.79%
1974	10.33%	14.0%	11.0%	-2.12%
1975	6.14%	14.0%	9.1%	-3.82%
1976	5.08%	14.0%	5.8%	-1.43%
1977	5.47%	14.0%	6.5%	-1.80%
1978	7.87%	14.0%	7.6%	-0.83%
1979	11.01%	14.0%	11.3%	-1.83%
1980	12.87%	14.0%	13.5%	-2.43%

*At bank

In 24 of the above 45 years, taxpayers in the LOWEST tax bracket had a negative return. While not shown above, taxpayers in the mid and top tax brackets lost 100% of their return almost 100% of the time.

What Things Cost				
Year	Newspaper	1st Class Stamp	Car	Home
1936	3¢	3¢	$695	$3,825
1937	3¢	3¢	$750	$4,000
1938	3¢	3¢	$753	$3,800
1939	3¢	3¢	$867	$3,700
1940	3¢	3¢	$828	$2,938
1941	3¢	3¢	$840	$2,938
1942	3¢	3¢	*	$3,529
1943	3¢	3¢	*	$3,868
1944	3¢	3¢	*	$4,238
1945	3¢	3¢	$1,030	$4,645
1946	3¢	3¢	$1,020	$5,080
1947	5¢	3¢	$1,200	$5,577
1948	5¢	3¢	$1,660	$6,112
1949	5¢	3¢	$1,362	$6,170
1950	5¢	3¢	$1,299	$7,354
1951	5¢	3¢	$1,362	$7,113
1952	5¢	3¢	$5,065	$8,090
1953	5¢	3¢	$2,679	$8,486
1954	5¢	3¢	$2,638	$8,901
1955	5¢	3¢	$2,395	$9,337
1956	5¢	3¢	$1,367	$9,795
1957	5¢	3¢	$1,467	$10,274
1958	5¢	4¢	$1,695	$10,777
1959	5¢	4¢	$1,561	$11,305
1960	6¢	4¢	$1,627	$11,900

*N/A WWII   Sources: W.V.H., Inc.; Annapolis Capital; Morris County Library; Department of Labor; Bureau of Labor Statistics; Board of Governors of the Federal Reserve System; U.S. Census Bureau

What Things Cost				
Year	News-paper	1st Class Stamp	Car	Home
1961	6¢	4¢	$2,464	$12,340
1962	7¢	4¢	$1,595	$12,797
1963	7¢	5¢	$2,494	$13,270
1964	7¢	5¢	$1,455	$13,761
1965	10¢	5¢	$1,959	$14,270
1966	10¢	5¢	$3,399	$14,798
1967	10¢	6¢	$2,365	$15,346
1968	10¢	6¢	$2,597	$15,913
1969	10¢	6¢	$3,175	$16,501
1970	10¢	6¢	$2,652	$17,000
1971	15¢	6¢	$3,395	$18,836
1972	15¢	8¢	$2,796	$20,870
1973	15¢	8¢	$4,281	$23,124
1974	15¢	8¢	$2,408	$25,621
1975	15¢	10¢	$2,999	$28,388
1976	20¢	13¢	$3,220	$31,454
1977	20¢	13¢	$3,588	$34,849
1978	20¢	13¢	$4,299	$38,613
1979	25¢	18¢	$10,654	$42,783
1980	25¢	15¢	$8,085	$47,200
1981	25¢	15¢	$6,194	$49,654
1982	25¢	20¢	$13,491	$52,236
1983	25¢	20¢	$9,399	$54,952
1984	25¢	20¢	$13,489	$57,810
1985	25¢	22¢	$8,999	$60,815

Sources: W.V.H., Inc.; Annapolis Capital; Morris County Library; Department of Labor; Bureau of Labor Statistics; Board of Governors of the Federal Reserve System; U.S. Census Bureau

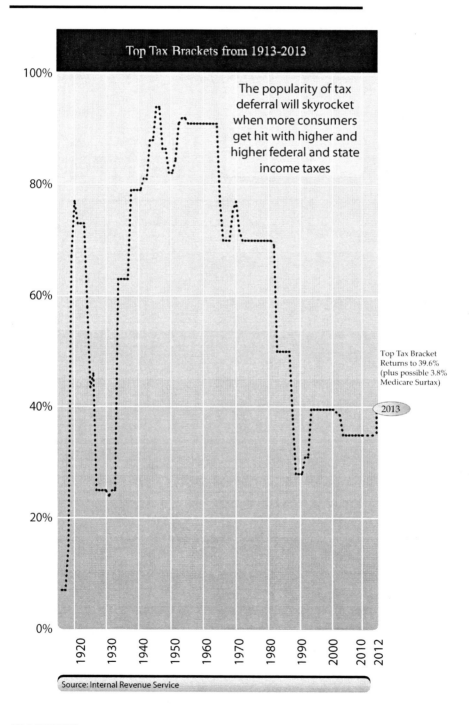

Top Tax Brackets from 1913-2013

The popularity of tax deferral will skyrocket when more consumers get hit with higher and higher federal and state income taxes

Top Tax Bracket Returns to 39.6% (plus possible 3.8% Medicare Surtax)

2013

Source: Internal Revenue Service

Index

Index

D

death benefit 120, 144, 248, 250, 267, 317, 329, 334, 341
divorcee 312
Dow Jones 72, 73, 178, 196, 278, 292, 293, 294, 329, 340, 346, 353
Dow Jones Industrial Average 72, 178, 196, 278, 294, 329, 340, 346, 353

E

EDIE 8, 309
Excess withdrawals x, 83, 84, 86

F

FDIC ix, ix–xv, ix–xv, xv, 1, 2, 3, 4, 5, 6, 8, 16, 17, 18, 19, 20, 24, 25, 26, 28,
       30, 32, 94, 144, 166, 170, 178, 185, 193, 194, 198, 246, 249, 253, 257,
       266, 267, 279, 283, 288, 295, 296, 298, 308, 309, 328, 6, 334, 335, 336,
       342, 343, 65
FDIC insured ix, xv, 1, 2, 4, 5, 6, 16, 18, 20, 24, 32, 94, 144, 170, 178, 194,
       266, 288, 295, 296, 298, 308, 309, 334, 343
financial pyramid xi, 111, 112, 114

G

Guaranteed Lifetime Withdrawal Benefit vii
guaranteed monthly income xiv, 176, 239, 242, 288, 240
guaranteed selling
price xiv
Guaranty Association 254

H

Heirs ix, 25, 26, 28, 54, 85

I

Immediate Annuities 134, 329, 337, 344
indexed annuities xv, 291, 292, 294
Inflation xi, 23, 95, 96, 97, 98, 103, 104, 105, 106, 180, 182, 189, 347, 352
inherited ix, 25, 26, 28
interest rate volatility ix, 9, 10, 12
IRA x, xiv, 54, 79, 80, 81, 82, 147, 148, 152, 155, 156, 176, x, 184, 185, 56,
       207, 219, 220, 222

L

Laddering CDs ix, 9, 10, 11, 12

M

market value adjustment 176, 232, 234, 290, 330, 331
match 67, 68, 70, 100, 102, 244
mentors xi, 40, 123, 124, 126, 134, 140
Modified Adjusted Gross Income vii
movies xi, 76, 84, 127, 128, 134, 214, 130
Multi-Year Guarantee Annuities 330, 331
Multi-Year Interest Rate 339, 342

N

new car xii, 17, 139, 140, 142

P

premature withdrawal penalties 144, 148
purchasing power xiii, 16, 123, 187, 188, 190, 346

Q

qualified annuity xiv, 176, 219, 220, 232, 316, 317, 222
qualified plan 80

R

real return 22, 346
Recharacterization 155, 156
Renewal Rates 342
riders 40, 273, 276, 329, 330, 339
ROTH Conversion xii, 155, 156, 158
ROTH IRA 54, x, 56, 156
Rule of 72 152
run on the bank xv, 30, 32, 269, 270, 272, 288, 339, 343

S

SEP 156, 164, 166
Simplified Employee Pension Plan 165
Social Security v, x, xi, xiii, 41, 42, 43, 44, 45, 46, 47, 48, 57, 58, 59, 60, 62, 119, 120, 122, 132, 179, 182, 211, 212, 213, 214, 311, 312, 337, 346, 349, 214, 122
Social Security Statement xi, 119, 120, 122
S&P 500® 291, 292, 294, 314
Standard & Poors 284, 294
Stepped-Up Cost basis 317
stock market 80, 259, 260, 277, 286, 314
Surrender charges xiv, xv, 269, 270, 272

Index

T

taxable equivalent yields 300
tax bracket vii, x, xi, 22, 49, 50, 52, 87, 88, 90, 180, 183, 186, 188, 193, 214,
    224, 295, 300, 309, 338
Tax-Deferred Annuities iv, xiii, xiv, xv, xvi, 225, 235, 236, 288, 315, 329, 330,
    331, 332, 337, 338, 339, 340, 341, 342, 343, 344
Taxes and inflation ix, 21, 22, 24
Tax-free xii, 143, 144, 146
Think about your money xii, 40, 135, 136, 138
Traditional Annuities 330, 331, 342

U

unallocated annuity 254, 267

V

variable annuities 40, 144, 208, 255, 260, 273, 316, 331, 342

W

what things cost 140, 141, 346
worse case
scenario xiv